Praise for *JOY, INC.*

"Richard Sheridan and Menlo Innovations have been making the future of software design come alive for a decade now. *Joy, Inc.* has the power to do the same for workplaces everywhere. Guaranteed to change the way you view life and business. Sheridan's writing makes clear that you really can have fun, make great products, and make a living all at the same time!"

—ARI WEINZWEIG, cofounder and CEO,
Zingerman's Community of Businesses, and author,
Zingerman's Guide to Good Leading Part 1: A Lapsed Anarchist's Approach to Building a Great Business

"Every single person working in business today needs to read this ground-breaking book. By bringing humanity back to business and focusing on producing not a merely a product but a joyful experience, Richard Sheridan has built an outstanding organization at Menlo. *Joy, Inc.* will show you how to tap into what may be the last frontier—and the first truly successful one—in building a high-performing organization."   —KAREN MARTIN, author,
The Outstanding Organization

"It's about time someone brought real joy to the world of work! Richard Sheridan has not only done it himself, he shows how you, too, can system-atically pursue a better workplace by offering a practical, joy-inducing idea on nearly every page. We urge you to bring joy into your business."

—JOE PINE and JIM GILMORE, coauthors,
The Experience Economy and *Authenticity*

"*Joy, Inc.* is a management book like no other: brilliant, fascinatingly told, and full of memorable and innovative ideas. It has the potential to revolutionize the way we work. Sheridan has proved that a system built around human needs actually works better by any metric you choose to apply, from produc-tivity to profitability to flexibility to sustainability. Thank you, Richard Sher-idan, for sharing your riches with us."   —JOHN GALL, author,
Systemantics, now in its third edition as *The Systems Bible*

"What makes this book such a compelling read is that Sheridan has actually done what he writes about—achieved joy and the business results that come from it—and shows how you can do it, too. I'm a busy guy and tried to skim through the pages. That didn't work; it's too good. This is an emphatic, dramatic, and pragmatic piece of writing. It deserves your attention, unless joy just isn't your thing."   —STAN SLAP, author,
Bury My Heart at Conference Room B

"If you suspect that joy and profit can be mutually reinforcing, this is the book for you. Richard Sheridan not only confirms that joy in your business is possible, he offers a plan for creating it in your own company."

—ROBERT QUINN, professor,
Ross School of Business, University of Michigan

"Richard Sheridan has created a contemporary business culture based on the best elements of Thomas Edison's invention factory. In *Joy, Inc.* he provides a guide for you to transform your workplace into a more creative and fulfilling place."

—MICHAEL J. GELB, author,
How to Think Like Leonardo da Vinci and
Innovate Like Edison

"Joy is the right word when talking about the creative and energetic work of Rich Sheridan and his impressive team at Menlo Innovations. *Joy, Inc.* shows you how a master innovator has created a joyous culture and the competencies necessary to make great work fun."

—JEFF DEGRAFF, professor,
Ross School of Business, University of Michigan,
and author, *Innovation You*

"Sheridan named his company after Thomas Edison's Menlo Park laboratory, and the lessons he provides in *Joy, Inc.* show how well he learned from Edison's example. From open spaces that encourage the constant sharing of information to an iterative design process that values frequent testing and a willingness to learn from failure, both Menlos prove that a workplace that values fun and joy can sustain a productive, innovative environment."

—PAUL ISRAEL, director and general editor,
Thomas A. Edison Papers, Rutgers University

"*Joy Inc.* is a joy to read, a joy to embrace, and a joy to practice. It's must reading for everyone who knows there has to be a better way to live your values at work. I couldn't put it down."

—JASON JENNINGS,
author of the *New York Times* bestsellers
The Reinventors and *Think Big, Act Small*

"Sheridan and I are kindred spirits in our quest to building the 'beloved' organization. *Joy, Inc.* shows you not only how to build a workplace that your team truly loves, but also how to pass that joy on to your clients and customers."

—JEANNE BLISS, author,
"I Love You More Than My Dog"

Joy, Inc.

Joy, Inc.

How We Built a Workplace
People Love

Richard Sheridan

PORTFOLIO / PENGUIN

PORTFOLIO / PENGUIN
Published by the Penguin Group
Penguin Group (USA) LLC
375 Hudson Street
New York, New York 10014

USA | Canada | UK | Ireland | Australia | New Zealand | India | South Africa | China
penguin.com
A Penguin Random House Company

First published by Portfolio / Penguin, a member of Penguin Group (USA) LLC, 2013

Photographs courtesy of the author

ISBN: 978-159184-587-4

Printed in the United States of America
5   7   9   10   8   6   4

Set in Adobe Garamond Pro
Designed by Elyse Strongin

Dedicated with love to

Carol, my pair partner in life,

and our beautiful girls,

Megan, Lauren, and Sarah.

And to James, my pair partner in work and golf.

You all are my joy!

Contents

Foreword

R ich Sheridan was close to writing the wrong book.
I stopped him dead in his tracks during the latest stages of his manuscript writing and implored him to change direction.

This wouldn't be a difficult change in what he'd already written to that point, but it was profoundly important for what he was going to say to the world.

The book he thought he was writing was *Joy, Inc.* The book he was almost going to send to the world could have been called *Change, Inc.*

Perhaps a good book, perhaps an important book, but not this book. Not the book I thought the world needed. Not the book I knew—from personal experience and from seeing his firm—that Rich was capable of writing. Not the book you all needed to read. Not the book that perhaps only Rich could write. In short, he was not about to write one of the most important business culture books of all time.

I told him it was time to take a stand.

For joy.

Too many business books do the same thing. They equivocate, they hedge, they apologize. They let you, the reader, off the hook and in the process they take away your hope—hope that things could be profoundly different than they are right now. This could have been that kind of business book. Quite frankly, I was going to do everything in my power to make sure that didn't happen. If I didn't, the world would be denied a very important message—one it is desperate to hear and needs to hear. It's also a message that Rich Sheridan, through a combination of his wiring, experience, and passion, is uniquely qualified to give you.

You see, when you tantalize readers with the notion of joy, and then tell them how to get there, that's a big promise. Everyone promises to help you change your culture. We've been writing about it for over three decades. I personally want to be Menlo. I want the joy. I told Rich, "I don't think you need to equivocate by suggesting that readers can pick the target they want." That message was unnecessarily tolerant. Crap—anyone can pick money, performance, or whatever. But *joy*—who's had the guts to promise that? To be honest, I'm sick to death of writers who don't take a stance.

The TV shows I watched as a boy typically opened with the scene of a business-suited father coming home from work at the end of the day, carrying an expensive briefcase and whistling a happy tune. As the inconsequential sitcom plot unfolded, there were no references to Dad's actual work "back at the office." No writer dared bring down the mood with sordid details about work. Consequently, the message of the fifties was as vague as it was odd. Work was a place that called for a suit and hat and required actions of a mysterious nature—that left employees whistling show tunes at the end of the day.

My own father painted a very different picture of his workplace. We watched our TV from the other side of the tracks. The people in our neighborhood wore thick aprons and gloves at work to keep the gunk, slime, and glue off their clothes. You didn't see Dad or any of our neighbors sporting a fedora any more than you spotted one of them whistling as he came home from work. And most certainly the woman next door, who worked at the fish cannery, didn't skip her way into her doily-adorned living room. After work, she went straight to the kitchen, where she tried her best to wash the stench of fish from her hands.

Given the circumstances on our side of the tracks, people complained endlessly about the backbreaking and mind-numbing nature of their jobs along with the stupidity and pettiness of their bosses. They hated their jobs. It's what they talked about. It's what they told jokes about. It's what they wrote songs about. To paraphrase a line from *City Slickers*, if my dad's hate for his job had been people, he'd have been China.

With this in mind, imagine my surprise some twenty years later when one day I found myself whistling as I walked out the door—on the way to work, no less. I loved what I did. I wore neither suit nor fedora, but somehow I had found a way to extract joy from my job. What a shock.

At first I thought my satisfaction at work stemmed from the fact that I had a career rather than a job. Not true. A couple of years later, as the exhilaration of first creating a nifty product of my very own gave way to managing the unrelenting demands of customers and employees who were both interdependent and at each other's throats, I learned that it wasn't the side of the tracks you worked on that determined your satisfaction. It was something else—something far more elusive. Working in a job you call a profession or in a building that's part of a "campus" or, for that matter, a mine chock-full of jewels doesn't necessarily lead to whistling as you skip along your path homeward. Joy doesn't spring from the nature of your product or service; it lies in the something else. But what?

Then I met Richard Sheridan. Four decades earlier, Rich had entered the field of software development, filled with the notion that creating software would be a genuine hoot. But then, like me, he learned that clients—no matter how cool the products or nifty the gadgets his firm was producing for them—changed their minds in mid-development, leading to ugly meetings with tons of finger-pointing and much gnashing of teeth. Code-writing employees became content experts who didn't dare take a day off work or, heaven forbid, leave on vacation, for fear of causing a costly intellectual vacuum in their absence.

What had started as a gentle romp down Candy Cane Lane was now a tortuous grind through the valley of unfulfilled expectations— the same valley I occasionally visited and was now trying to avoid. Where had we gone wrong? Better yet, how could we return our firms to places that left us with a spring in our step and a tune on our lips?

Rich had the answer. While I plowed away at creating interpersonal training, he studied joy and worked it into his company, and now all of those insights are in this book. I visited his place of work and hung on his every word. It was amazing to watch people eagerly creating, collaborating, and interfacing with customers, brainstorming in teams, and eventually meeting harsh deadlines and demanding product specs—all with a clear sense of passion and accomplishment.

A few months passed while I tried to implement what I had learned from Rich back at my place of work. One day, he sent me an e-mail informing me that his new book was coming out soon and it would focus on how to shape an organization's culture, with some emphasis on shaping it into a joyous workplace. The primary message would be that you could choose whatever type of organization you wanted and shape it into that. The point would be that you had to be intentional about your culture.

What? Had Rich gone mad? So I wrote him the following:

```
Rich, your book needs to have one message. If you're
going to call the book Joy, Inc. it can't be a book
that says you can create whatever corporate culture
you want and here's how. Everyone promises to help
you change your culture. I personally want the joy
you allude to in the title, and what I saw firsthand.
```

I went on to tell Rich,

> Your voice is the voice of hope, followed by the
> voice of practical wisdom. For the love of Mike,
> don't stop short of telling people to seek a culture
> of joy. You're being far too modest by hinting they
> can choose whatever. Somebody needs to stand up for
> joy. Please consider it your calling. Please don't
> equivocate your way into another book on culture
> change. Anything that steps off the stance of "Joy
> is the purpose and here's how to get it" lessens
> your message, raises doubt in the reader, and
> throws the title into question.

I was successful in my exhortations. *Joy, Inc.* is the book you need to read. *Joy, Inc.* takes a stand—for joy in the workplace.

It's about darn time.

KERRY PATTERSON
Cofounder, VitalSmarts
Author, *Influencer, Crucial Conversations,*
Crucial Confrontations, Change Anything

Joy, Inc.

Why Joy?

Joy in business sounds ridiculous. Perhaps that's why, early on, I hedged on writing about building a culture of joy, why I was tempted to equivocate.

Joy is a pie-in-the-sky, cymbals-clanging, music-playing, radical dream. *Joy* is a word that carries connotations of love, happiness, health, purpose, and values. Joy might work at home, or at church, or with a hobby—but not at the office. It's a concept that has no place in the corporate world. It certainly does not sound profitable.

It may sound radical, unconventional, and bordering on being a crazy business idea. However—as ridiculous as it sounds—joy is the core belief of our workplace. Joy is the reason my company, Menlo Innovations, a custom software design and development firm in Ann Arbor, exists. It defines what we do and how we do it. It's the single shared belief of our entire team. And joy is what brought you to me.

You see, I know why you're reading this book. It's because you are hoping, somewhat beyond hope, to bring joy into your own workplace.

Deep down you *know* that there is a better way to run a business, a team, a company, a department. You've always known it. These thoughts come to you just before falling asleep or just after waking.

Then your day begins, and the idea of transformational change evaporates like a maddening dream you can't seem to reassemble after waking from it.

Although you may be silently (or not so silently) tortured in your current broken company culture, you haven't given up completely. Change is still possible.

I was in the same place once—deeply unsatisfied with my work and my own ability to do anything about it. But things can be better. My company, Menlo Innovations, has captured joy and made it true and sustainable for everyone who works with us and for us. In this book, I will give you a good look into the radical practices we employ at Menlo that make our work such a unique experience. I'll also share my personal journey from youthful joy to deep disillusionment to endless optimism in a workplace of joy.

Imagine Joy

Setting out to intentionally design and transform an organization is a monumental task. And yet you must have an idea of what your dream company would look like and how it would run. If your company could look like anything you wanted, what one word would describe the resulting organization?

> Successful?
> Profitable?
> Energized?
> Fun?
> Fulfilling?
> Productive?
> Dominant?

Innovative?

Engaged?

How about *joyful*?

If you assemble a team of human beings to create something new and compelling, joy can be described quite simply:

Joy is designing and building something that actually sees the light of day and is enjoyably used and widely adopted by the people for whom it was intended.

Tangible joy means delivering a product or service to the world that's so enjoyed, in fact, that people stop you on the street and say, "Really, you did that? I *love* it." If you can accomplish this outcome while elevating the spirit of the hardworking team, you will have achieved a result that most companies only dream about.

Menlo Innovations, my version of a joyful company, is on a personally selfish yet noble journey. I desperately wanted to work in a joyful place with joyful people achieving joyful outcomes. I wanted to have fun at work while producing wonderful results within a sustainable business.

My first serious pursuit of joy came as vice president of R&D at a public company where, for two years, I achieved the culture I was seeking—before the Internet bubble burst and took it all away. What I learned in those two years became the prototype for what would become Menlo Innovations in 2001.

Since its founding, Menlo has grown steadily. We've won five *Inc.* magazine growth awards, tripled our physical office three times, and produced products that dominate markets for our clients. We've also received quite a bit of notice for our unique culture, have been recognized as one of the ten happiest places to work on the planet by the Chief Happiness Officer in Denmark, and were named one of 2013's twenty-five most audacious small companies by *Inc.* magazine. Menlo is noted annually as one of the world's Most Democratic Workplaces by WorldBlu, founded by Traci Fenton.

Every year, thousands of people come from all over the world just to visit Menlo and experience our culture firsthand. And I sleep well every night, knowing I have personally achieved the joy I sought, within a company that has been profitable every year without any outside investment. Our countercultural approach is not complicated, although getting to simple is almost never easy.

Joy? You're Kidding

Joy is not a word often associated with business success. This is particularly true in my industry: designing, building, launching, and maintaining complex software. The software industry, after all, defined the term "death march" in a business context: programmers pulling all-nighters, bringing sleeping bags to work, jettisoning time with loved ones, canceling vacations. These death marches often lead to the saddest story of all: projects canceled before they ever see the light of day. The programmers look back over the litter of their personal lives and wonder why they put in so much effort.

That same software industry also foisted on the world the idea that users are stupid. Those "stupid users" will need *Dummies* books to help them successfully use our beautifully designed technology because they're not smart enough to comprehend what we've built. Our industry taught the world to accept awful programming errors and gaping security holes as a natural outcome of technological progress.

I know this as well as anyone. After an incredibly hopeful beginning, for most of my career I was as far from joy as you could get. As I advanced from a programmer in the trenches to an executive of a high-flying public company, I was an active member of those death marches. I was burning out and had difficulty sleeping at night as I wrestled with customer promises that couldn't be kept and the demands I placed on my team. We shipped poor-quality products that offered mountains of trouble for the users. When I voiced my concerns, executive peers assured me that there would be plenty of time to fix problems after delivery. I never saw that promise come true. When abundant problems did arrive as predicted, my bosses told me they never asked me to create such crappy products.

I used to think it was just me and that everyone else was doing okay. Now I know I was not alone. So many people now reach out to me to see how they can bring joy into their workplaces: health care systems, schools, colleges, churches, nonprofits, automotive companies, medical equipment manufacturers. I also hear from some of the highest-flying companies on the planet, companies that win awards for their cultures. Even they haven't found joy.

It doesn't have to be that way. In our pursuit of this elusive joy, Menlo has changed *everything* about our approach and our process—and along the way, turned traditional ideas about management and culture and sustainability on their head. From our radical changes, we've developed lessons that can be applied to any organization, not just software teams. I hope our experience with building joy into the core of our business inspires you to seek the change you have always hoped was possible.

In the following pages, we'll explore disciplines that executive management can use to bring joy into their own work environments: simple, repeatable processes that actually feed into predictable outcomes; powerful human resources management without traditional HR; products designed specifically for the intended consumers; and quality practices that ensure the phone never rings with problems. *Joy, Inc.* will teach you about implementing structure without bureaucracy and making decisions without meetings. You will learn about the effect of removing "manufactured fear" from the workplace and how to build human energy by removing ambiguity. We'll also look at preserving basic human principles such as dignity, teamwork, discipline, trust, and joy.

While I use many examples from my own journey, it is not my intention to suggest that the way we do things at my company is exactly the way you should do things at yours. I have, however, learned over the years that tangible examples can be very helpful, and yet they are rare in business books. I have lived the stories in this book over a career that has spanned more than forty years. This book is intended as experiential storytelling, meant to encourage and inspire because, all too often, leading cultural change is a very lonely pursuit.

We are lucky to host many smart, conscientious academics who come to visit our company to see firsthand what we have created. They often espouse theories of why Menlo works, and are puzzled when they find out we didn't develop our practices by first deeply studying the more complex theories of organizational design and teamwork. For Menlo, building a culture of joy was simple: we wanted to create a place where we were excited to come to work every day.

A Joyful Culture Is Shared

A joyful culture draws in people from outside the company, including clients, the local community, and the press. A cornerstone of Menlo's success is our ability to pass along our ideas and practices to others.

In 2012 alone, we hosted 241 separate tour groups, totaling 2,193 visitors. These visitors came from all around the world to visit the basement of a parking structure in downtown Ann Arbor in what many consider to be the flyover zone of the United States. The tours are promoted almost entirely by word of mouth; we don't advertise the tours, other than with a passing mention on our Web site. Some are paid, but most are free. I personally lead many of them. The visitors come seeking what I was searching for so many years before and what you are seeking now.

When I lead tours, I start by saying, "Welcome to Menlo, a place that has created an intentional culture focused on the *business value of joy*."

Visitors are often stunned to hear Menlo described this way. They believe that we are an interesting software company, and by visiting us they might gain some clever takeaways that can help their own technical team. But once they are here, they are confronted by joy that is so tangible and out front it is impossible to avoid. Our version of joy in business has implications for a much wider audience within their own company, regardless of industry.

Why does *joy* need to be the focus?

"Well," I ask visitors, "what do you think would happen if half the Menlo team had joy and half didn't? Which half would you want us to assign to your imagined project?"

Of course, they always pick the joyful half of my team.

"But why would you want the joyful half of my team?" I ask. "What difference would that make?"

Answers come pouring out:

"They'd be more productive."

"They'd be more engaged."

"They'd be easier to work with."

"They'd do better work."

"They'd care more about the outcome."

Anyone can quickly and easily recognize that a joyful team will produce better outcomes. And our joy is not only internal. Our focus is to ensure that the work we do in this room gets out into the world, to be widely adopted and delightfully used by large numbers of the intended audience. A joyful company cares deeply about the change it is making in the world. You can't sustainably achieve that outside joy unless there is also inside joy.

With this book, I invite you, too, to peek inside our doors at Menlo and see what joy can look like. Feel the energy of a space that is wide open, flexible, and devoid of physical barriers to human communication. Hear the team at work, as pairs of people engage in active and animated conversations. See the walls covered with paper and yarn, pushpins and colorful sticky dots. Learn everything you can about how we created our *Joy, Inc.* and search, along with us, for answers to the following questions:

What is an intentionally joyful culture?
How do you reinvent a broken culture and get to joy?
Can you do this while being profitable?

Joy Will Lift You and Your Team

The principles that drive human organizations are similar to those that lift airplanes off the ground. Think of the contrast between modern flying machines and the failed attempts of ancient man. In my early career, I tried the managerial equivalent of those, like those in ancient times, who strapped on feathered wings and flapped with all their might, yet never succeeded in getting airborne. I accomplished little despite all the effort, and became tired and frustrated.

We all know that the Wright brothers broke through and flew— but *why* were they the first to succeed where myriad men had failed? They also had plenty of stiff competition among their contemporaries, including Samuel Pierpont Langley. Langley led a well-funded,

highly educated team of scientists in the race to build the first powered, manned airplane. It lost the flight race to the Wright brothers,
who were total unknowns at the time, and promptly quit any further
exploration into flight.

There are many theories about why the Wright brothers were able
to fly and Langley was not. I have a simple one.

Langley was trying to build an airplane. The Wright brothers
wanted to fly.

Langley was pursuing history, glory, and financial rewards. The
Wright brothers were pursuing joy. They wanted to fly and see the
world as the birds do. (Having gotten my pilot's license when I was
nineteen years old, I fully appreciate the joy of powered flight.)
Their pursuit of joy, of one concrete ideal, made the difference in
their victory. It was one of the reasons I was so unfulfilled in my
early management career. I was flapping my wings the way I had
seen my own bosses do, but to what end? I wasn't quite sure.

I now know what I want in business: joy. A pursuit of joy within
a business context is not about the pursuit of fame or profit. Humans aspire to a higher purpose. Teams desire to work on goals
bigger than themselves. They want to have a lasting and valued effect on the world. They want to make their mark, not for the glory,
but for the purpose of bringing delight or ending suffering. Like the
Wright brothers, we at Menlo want to fly. We've found that profit,
fame, and glory often follow us in this path, too.

Happiness and Joy Are Not the Same

In this exploration of joy, I avoid the temptation to go down the
happiness route. There is nothing wrong with happiness, and there
is no question you should also seek happiness. It's just that joy is

deeper, more meaningful, and purposeful. Happiness is more a momentary state of being. You can be joyful without being happy every moment.

At Menlo, we have fun, we laugh a lot, and there is almost always palpable energy—but we aren't always happy. We have a shared belief system. We are focused and driven. At times, we are cynical and sometimes downright angry. We use the energy of our anger and cynicism to fuel our work, in hopes of ending the human suffering caused by what is perhaps one of the most broken industries on the planet: information technology.

Like you, what we do is challenging and important. For example, our team cocreated one of the world's leading cancer and AIDS research instruments and collaborated on building a comprehensive organ transplant information system. With these projects, our company did important, meaningful work that was years in the making. It would be hard to be happy the entire time. In fact, if happiness was a requirement for success, we would have stopped very early on when the going got too tough. The focus on a tangible, joyful outcome is what kept us going then and still does.

Joy is the deep satisfaction you get from successfully training for and completing a marathon.

Joy is watching your daughter marry the man of her dreams, knowing that all the exhausting work of parenting is expressed in a simple "I do."

Joy is the feeling a fighter pilot gets when, after all the training and preparation, she lands an F-18 on the deck of an aircraft carrier in rough seas, strong winds, and low visibility. Once the engine is quiet and the wheels secured, she knows that the aircraft, the carrier, the flight deck team, and she are all safe and sound—and she can't wait to do it again.

We all want joy in our work lives, in our downtime, in our kids' schools, in our faith communities, in our families, and in our nation. Humans are wired to work on things bigger than themselves, to be in community with one another. It's why we join teams and companies, and work very hard and long to achieve a difficult and elusive shared goal.

This fundamental and intrinsically motivating pursuit of joy is why you are reading this book.

———————

Welcome to Joy, Inc.

I'm so glad you are here.

My Journey to Joy

It was early September in 1971 when I first fell in love.

I was only a freshman in high school, but a singular moment changed the course of my life. My love was not for a girl; that would come a few years later. This love was for a magical machine.

I sat down at a Teletype and typed in a two-line program:

```
10 PRINT "HI RICH"
20 END
```

Then I typed:

```
RUN
```

The computer responded by typing back:

```
HI RICH
```

I was hooked and instantly knew what I was going to do for the rest of my life. I was going to be an artist. My medium? Software. It was the ultimate sculpting material. At only thirteen years old, I had already identified a life purpose, an important heart song. This was my first hint of joy.

The next year, after school and around homework, I labored into the night to create a program that would now be called "Fantasy Baseball." I just wanted to keep playing the game I loved with my friends during long Michigan winters. I came up with the rules of the game and typed the entire official *Baseball Register* into the computer. More than five hundred of my childhood baseball heroes' lifetime statistics, their positions, and whether they batted or pitched right or left—all typed in. The program let us pick our teams, select our lineups, and play them against one another. The delight I felt as my friends and I played this computer game together reinforced my purpose. With the encouragement of my teacher and lovingly supported by my mom and dad, I entered that program into an international programming contest and won in the gaming category.

That competitive technological achievement landed me my first job as a programmer before I could drive: working for the computer-based instruction department of the Macomb Intermediate School District in Michigan, using the same computers that had hooked me in those first wonderful moments of my freshman year of high school. I led the creation of the first e-mail system Macomb County schools ever saw. We grew a big team of high school programmers who worked every waking minute just to be a part of this revolution. The spirit, energy, and camaraderie of a young team of peers learning and experimenting together was intoxicating. The adults around us had no idea exactly what we were doing. To them we looked like child prodigies and technical heroes, which just added to the headiness of it. Above all, I couldn't believe I was being paid to do the thing I just loved to do as a hobby.

The Slide from Joy to Fear

Through high school and college, my personal fire was burning bright. I was excited both about my own future and the world's; the computer was going to change everything, and software was the magic that made it all work. I was going to be part of a movement as important as anything man had ever discovered: fire, the wheel, electricity, film, mass production, television, transistors, integrated circuits. In pursuit of my career aspirations, I eventually earned two degrees from the University of Michigan in computer science and engineering.

By all external measures, the career that followed was perfect. Every year brought promotions, raises, stock options, greater responsibilities, and bigger offices. Between 1982 and 1997, I advanced from programmer to vice president as I worked my way through a handful of local Ann Arbor technology companies. I spent the majority of my career at Interface Systems, Inc. By 1999, Interface was the number one public company in Michigan based on stock growth. My stock options were worth over $4 million. I had everything I thought I had wanted as a kid, or so it seemed.

Yet at the midpoint of this career rise, I wanted out. My chosen field had betrayed me. I was in a trough of disillusionment, trapped in a career that had no joy, and I couldn't leave.

On the outside, I was still viewed as a great success, grabbing promotions and raises and greater responsibilities. But although I was still succeeding in the eyes of the world, that didn't matter to me anymore, as I stared daily at my life of quiet desperation. There were long nights and weekends away from the family I loved, for me and the people who worked for me. Vacations were impossible to schedule. Projects were always in trouble, and then they were canceled. Disappointed colleagues yelled during difficult meetings. I believed that the only way out of my management quagmire was to fire half the team, but I hated the hiring process, so that, too, seemed like a dead end. Quality issues delayed deployments. Customers complained incessantly about the delays and the results.

My patience and love for the software game seemed to be finite after all. I had two choices: change the industry or get out.

I chose change.

In 1997, at forty years old, I was promoted to vice president of research and development of Interface by then CEO Bob Nero, an outsider who had only recently taken over the leadership role. For years before Bob's arrival, I had lived in fear of my organization and I certainly didn't want to sign up for the uncapped personal commitment that came with the executive seat of a public company. While Bob's informal research with my peers had confirmed that I possessed the knowledge, experience, and trust of the organization, I resisted the promotion. No way in hell was I going to accept his offer of an executive seat, despite the obvious potential financial rewards.

My rejection angered Bob, since I was the key player in his plans to turn around the company he was now captaining. He threw me out of his office.

At home that evening, I sat down and really thought about his offer and the options before me. I reflected on my deep love for this profession. I recalled that intense joy of discovery I felt when I first laid hands on that Teletype keyboard. Settling into this introspection, I also reminisced about a dream I'd had during my college days at Michigan: that I would one day build the best damn software team that Ann Arbor had ever seen.

I realized I was in a race I had never expected. My personal flame was going out; my life outside of work was becoming the salve for a broken life inside of work. There were a couple of years, just before Bob Nero's arrival on the scene, when I would take long drives through backcountry roads in order to arrive at work as late as possible, then spend half my day playing FreeCell with my screen turned away from the door. I had stopped caring.

All of this went through my mind that evening after being angrily thrown out of Bob's office. I made a decision that night to pursue deep, lasting change and to find a way to love my job and my industry once again—and make it better.

There had to be a better way to do things, a better way to work and manage a team. Though I had no firm idea what I was looking for, I was convinced there was a solution out there for my existential crisis and that I'd know it when I saw it. I thought back to the software engineering classes I'd taken in my college days at Michigan, and my occasional envious peeks at high-performing collaborative software teams such as Data Connection Ltd. in the UK.

Over the years, I had also read numerous books on organizational design and management principles. That night I reflected on some of those that had influenced me the most, such as Peter Senge's *The Fifth Discipline*, Peter Drucker's *Management*, Tom Peters's *In Search of Excellence*, and John Naisbitt's *Megatrends*. Perhaps like many business books you may have read, these were as frustrating to me as they were inspiring. They described great organizations, but they didn't tell you how to build one.

One thing I realized I had in my favor, however, was that I am by nature an eternal optimist, as well as being persistent. Put me in a room full of manure and I will keep digging until I find the pony. It was time to finally apply everything I had learned and thought about during my years of searching. This was my moment.

The very next day, I told Bob that I would take the promotion and use the new role to build that "best damn software team." Bob was very surprised by the 180-degree turnaround in one evening, but he was supportive of my renewed vigor. I'm sure neither of us knew at the time how far this journey was going to take us.

What I did know was that it wasn't going to be easy. One particularly poignant moment in signing up for this greater responsibility was a parking lot conversation I had with Kimberly, a very talented leader who would now be working for me.

"Congratulations on your promotion to VP," Kimberly began. "Couldn't have happened to a nicer guy."

While her congratulations were sincere, I knew exactly what she meant. *Nice won't cut it here; you'll be eaten alive. Good luck with that.* I felt her good wishes in the pit of my stomach.

The next two years were the beginning of a journey back to self. Once again, I began to live out my personal values at work. I spent more time with each member of my team, getting to know his or her hopes and desires for the future and sharing mine. I kept an open channel of communication about what was going on at the executive level, and made individual expectations clearer for the work that was needed. Things got better quickly but were still nowhere near good enough.

Renewed personal energy simply wasn't going to transform a whole culture. I needed something more: an entirely new approach, a framework for this improved organization.

Joy Again: My "Click Moment"

In 1999, after two years of intense searching for a better way to work and hold a team, two significant discoveries happened within weeks of one another. The first of these was a wiki (an early form of blogging) I began reading by a guy named Kent Beck, who would soon publish a book on what he called "Extreme Programming." Beck described a radical approach to software programming based on dramatic change: opening up your work space, managing projects with handwritten note cards, breaking big projects down into shorter, measurable cycles, and getting your team to work in pairs.

A few weeks after reading Beck's wiki, I tuned in to a *Nightline* episode about IDEO, the famous industrial design company in Palo Alto. In watching the thirty-minute segment, I saw a tangible example of what Beck meant by Extreme Programming. IDEO's style wasn't a perfect example of Beck's approach, but it was a company with enthusiasm, close collaborative teamwork, superb customer connection, and conscious design thinking.

Both Beck's book and the IDEO video outlined ways to connect with customers and end users in a real way by getting them directly involved with the work. In contrast, my team usually got information second- and thirdhand from the marketing team. We built software to its shadows-on-the-wall specifications, which were never entirely thought through and would change dramatically many times during the process. We never delivered what the market really needed.

But now I knew the workplace could be within reach. The search for a model of a joyful organization was officially over. I had a user manual and a video.

I shared the *Nightline* video with my colleagues on the executive team of this tired old public company and told them, "This is what I am going to do." (I was lucky they humored me for thirty minutes while we watched the video.) They were as excited by the possibilities of a new system as I was. When my harshest critic asked, "How soon do we knock down the walls?" I knew we were good to go. The board was in. My boss was in. They were all in.

Although I wasn't exactly certain how this transformation was going to work, I had two elements working in my favor. First, after having nearly gone out completely, my personal flame was starting to burn bright again. I began to believe again.

Far more critical to the success of radical workplace reimagining was having James Goebel on my side. Like many of the momentous elements in my journey to joy, meeting James was relatively random and, at first, seemingly unimportant. He was one of the lead consultants for the local Ann Arbor firm Appnet, which I'd contracted to train my team in a new approach to software development. James was assigned to my account and would be with me through this technical transformation. He had brought along a few expert Appnet programmers who would be used as side-by-side guides for my team.

James had never met anyone quite like me, someone willing to run lots of serious and radical experiments. Likewise, I had never met anyone like James, someone with the capacity to suggest crazy and exciting new ideas over and over again. He would be my partner through the change initiatives.

I had the CEO. I had the board. I had a partner. There was only one constituency left to get on board: my team of programmers.

Blood, Mayhem, Murder

My team knew I had been searching for new approaches to solve some of our most pressing problems. The problems, after all, were evident to everyone. Deadlines passed without working software or anything even close to a completed program. When the software was supposedly finished, the quality team couldn't even get it to work! The programmers who had already moved on to the next project declared, "It worked on my machine," and left it at that. When programs did finally work after months of quality testing, the results were seldom close to what the customers actually needed. Even if it was what they required, users didn't understand how to use it, so updated user documentation and training were then added to get the "stupid users" farther along the learning curve.

I gathered my team of fourteen software engineers and told them about this Extreme Programming stuff. These ideas were completely new to them and, quite frankly, shockingly different from anything they had experienced or contemplated.

"What do you think of all this?" I asked.

I was met with total silence.

My team had instantly sensed the danger. *Vice President Rich is considering something insane, and he just might try to do it if we don't kill this idea before it gets legs.*

"What do you think?" I asked again.

More silence. *Dead* silence.

Finally, Gyl raised his hand.

"Gyl, what do you think?"

"Blood, mayhem, murder," he said calmly but with solid conviction. "Don't do it, Rich. Don't make us do it. Don't pull us out of our offices. Don't make me share a computer. And please, *please* don't make me share my code. It's my code," he implored.

"Gyl, the last time I checked, we are a public company," I responded. "I think the code belongs to the shareholders."

"Whatever, Rich. It's my code."

Oh, my. This was not going to be easy.

The First Experiment

After that difficult meeting, Bob J. and Clare, two seasoned developers, approached me. They wanted to try this Extreme Programming experiment and give my wild idea a whirl.

Over the previous two years, I had authorized Clare to lead a by then failed change effort we had affectionately dubbed "Software Development Life Cycle" (SDLC). In our industry, we refer to this style of working as the waterfall approach. The process involved a central rules committee, prescribed meetings, mandatory executive sign-offs, stage gates with go/no go decision points, myriad standing committees to review in-progress documents, and on and on.

After the first project attempted to painfully pass through the full waterfall cycle, we decided we needed an SDLC-lite version so that quicker, shorter projects could be done without as much fanfare. But within months, the SDLC and its undernourished child, SDLC-lite, died a quiet death. We just never remembered to schedule the required meetings that no one would attend anyway. Clare became discouraged, as this new project style was his baby. His flame was going out just like mine.

You may have seen crushing bureaucracy enter your own organization through poorly informed implementations of management styles such as Lean, Six Sigma, or ISO. Or likely you've just seen an increase in process and procedure to try to get things under control: more meetings, more committees, or just more levels of hierarchy. These well-intentioned efforts typically increase cost, workload, and paperwork but have no material impact on quality, productivity, or improved communication.

As the SDLC efforts had expired—and since Clare and Bob J. were willing—I quickly authorized the Extreme Programming experiment that they suggested. The two of them immediately grabbed an "open lab" (a small, open room) as their work space. There, they sat side by side at a single computer, wrote automated unit tests, worked from handwritten index cards, and organized and reviewed their work in a planning game each week. In short, they tested Extreme Programming in the extreme, adapting all the techniques that Gyl and most of his colleagues had dismissed out of hand.

About three weeks into this experiment, Clare stopped me in the parking lot and asked if I was still going to pay him to work there.

"What do you mean?" I asked.

"I am having so much fun, it doesn't feel like work anymore," he replied. "I'm not sure you should pay me."

Just a few short weeks before this experiment, Clare had asked me to be a reference in his job search, as he had decided to leave the company. Clearly, with this new experiment, we had hit pay dirt.

"Blood, mayhem, murder" on one side. "I will work for you for free" on the other side. I was not getting lukewarm reactions. This was an M-curve reaction: extreme feelings on either side of the issue. I've come to realize that, in the face of a significant change initiative, emotional reactions fitting a standard bell curve will likely never create lasting change. You need the energy from the edges, not the middle.

The *Where* Is Just as Important as the *What*

It was excellent that Clare and Bob J. were on board, but I needed to build up this effort. I was convinced that a key to my imagined transformation of our entire organization would be the physical space. But where could we set up a wide-open space like the one Beck recommended and the IDEO video evoked? James and I were constrained by the stifling cubes and offices of my very traditional R&D division at thirty-year-old Interface Systems. The time and expense of remodeling was out of the question.

One morning, James approached me, electrified. He walked me out into the old factory space where Interface used to build printers. Pointing to the darkened, empty factory filled with cardboard boxes and mothballed assembly-line equipment, he said, "This is it."

I was not amused. This was a big, ugly room. A great big *open* ugly room. A wide-open space with no walls, offices, cubes, or doors. A giant, open, collaborative work space. This could be it! We commandeered the factory.

The Second Experiment

We prepared the factory space James had discovered: dismantled the production line, emptied out the stored equipment, hosed the whole space down. In its place, we installed simple eight-foot folding tables and chairs and hooked up a new electrical system appropriate for desktop computers. Now, how to entice the team into this new space?

James suggested an experiment. "Let's use the factory for deeper hands-on training in the new language of the Internet called Java," he said. We decided to teach fourteen of them using all these crazy new Extreme Programming techniques of pair programming, unit testing, and code stewardship that I had been discussing with the team. James's three consultant programmers would pair with mine. We would work this way for just a week, switching the pairs every day, so that every one of the team members would have a shot at working with James's consultant programmers for cross-training.

This time, there were no "blood, mayhem, murder" reactions, for two reasons. First, we would run this experiment for only a week. How bad could it be to work differently for five days? Second, we were giving the programmers an opportunity to learn Java, the latest technological shiny object. In 1999, every programmer in the nation wanted to learn Java.

I couldn't believe what I saw immediately in this new space: energy, noise, collaboration, progress, work, learning, and fun. In a word: joy. (Although I wouldn't think of it in those terms until years later.)

During the weeklong experiment, the rest of the company came, one by one and in small groups, to peek into our makeshift work space. The whole company buzzed about it. One of my guys, Tim, brought in a hard hat and put a sign on the door that read: "Java Factory: Hard Hats Required." We started calling it the Java Factory that week. The whimsical irreverence that would one day become standard fare was already beginning to emerge.

As you consider your own aspirations for cultural change, don't lose sight of how important it is to draw others into the energy and excitement. I have seen many teams attempt to "black box" change initiatives by hiding significant work style or organizational changes from their stakeholders. These initiatives usually die a quick death when the person leading the change is replaced.

A Critical Test of Leadership

At the end of the week, I gathered our test group together and asked the members what they thought of the training. The praise flowed:

"Wow, that was fun."

"I can't believe how much I learned."

"I can't believe how much we got done. Especially considering we really didn't even know Java at the beginning of the week."

Something momentous had just happened, a reaction I had been seeking for at least a decade. My next step would be critical. I had two choices: I could let the team go back to work in the usual way or seize the moment and keep running this obviously successful experiment.

You can probably guess what I chose.

"Great, guys," I said. "This is the way we are going to work from now on."

Once again, I was met with dead silence.

Then, in horror and in unison, they shouted, "No!"

I was hit full force with the biggest obstacle to change: fear of the unknown. The team members now knew more about what such a change would entail, but they still desperately wished to hold on to their old, comfortable ways. The experiment was fine for a week of training, but the implications of Extreme Programming as an everyday work style were more transformational than they were ready for.

I reminded the programming team that, a moment earlier, they had reacted positively to the experiment. Many programmers cast their eyes downward, realizing the contradiction they had presented, not only to me but also to themselves. They were torn on what to do.

"Guys, listen to what you just told me," I said. "'Never got more done. Never had so much fun. Never learned so much.' This is the way it's going to be from now on."

Many of the fourteen were none too happy with my declaration. Within days, some of my old-timers tried to end around me by attempting to convince the other execs this would never work. Some even approached board members they knew well. But it was too late on all those fronts, as I had pre-sold all of my executive VP peers, my boss, the board, and even a couple of major stockholders on our new way of working. We were on our way.

Change Isn't Easy

Change is never easy, but I wasn't looking for easy change. I was looking for meaningful change. I intrinsically understood what organizational change author Jeanenne LaMarsh teaches in her many books, including *Changing the Way We Change*. In order to get others to accept change, you must recognize that any change involves tearing down existing reward systems, especially if those reward systems unintentionally foster and perpetuate pain-filled systems. If the change is to stick, you must quickly replace the old rewards with new rewards of equal or greater value (and remember, most treasured rewards are not monetary). Failure to establish new rewards will cause the team to revert to old forms and old rewards the first chance they get.

What were my old team members' existing rewards?

- Code they could proudly claim as their own
- A good understanding of their *individual* contribution to company goals

- Performance reviews and raises and future goals focused on the above
- Private and personalized offices with doors that closed
- Library quiet so they could think deep thoughts
- Monitors turned away from the door
- Total autonomy from having to answer to their peers
- The ability to focus on the fun, hard, technical stuff
- Knowing that quality assurance was someone else's problem

What were the potential new rewards of this brand-new approach?

- Products that worked and shipped on time without drama
- Offerings that would be enjoyably used by the target users
- Belonging to a real team rather than just a department on an org chart
- The opportunity to learn something new every day
- Easily scheduled vacations without fear of being called while away
- No technical disasters needing heroic all-night recovery efforts
- Pride in a job well done
- No one perennially trapped in a tower of knowledge
- Not watching all the plum new assignments going to the new guys
- The feeling of actually being supported by their peers
- A sustainable approach that would repeatedly produce quality results
- An unprecedented level of engagement with the business
- A department of "Embrace change" rather than "No and slow"
- Fun. Energy. Excitement. Everything we really wanted from this profession

- And with a little bit of luck, rising stock option value based on real and tangible increasing business value of what they and the company did for a living

A New Day

I had firmly decided that the new Extreme Programming way was how we would work from now on. Though that team had convenient excuses to hide from change, the ace in my hand was Java. So James and I declared that if any of our programmers wanted to play any of the new reindeer games, including working on the new architecture and the new product line in Java, they had to work in the new way and in the new space.

This proclamation had the desired effect. My team began to volunteer less for old work. They wanted to play with their new toy—and it was worth working in the new style to do so. New patterns of physical movement began to emerge as some members of my team now stopped in at the Java Factory first thing in the morning instead of going to their individual, assigned workstations. After six months, Extreme Programming at Interface finally hit a tipping point where team members started to tell me they didn't need their old offices or cubes anymore.

Everyday work wasn't the only thing that changed. Status reporting also morphed. We were working in two-week cycles at the time, and every two weeks we would report our status in a fairly well-orchestrated event we came to call "Show & Tell." The entire company was invited to this event, at which my team presented what it had worked on. The business folks began to expect it and would set aside time on their schedules to attend. They felt they were an important part of the process. Secretaries, support teams, even the receptionist would come not only to see my team's energy but to learn more about what our company did for its customers. We began to make the business more understandable for everyone.

For the first time ever, the business executives had real, visible insight into what my technical team was doing and how far along we actually were. We had successfully built a bridge from R&D to the business. My team members began to sense the excitement and would get playful during Show & Tell. They would bring candy and toss it out in the crowd to anyone who asked questions. In one particularly memorable Show & Tell, the team set up an entire band, with drums, guitars, and microphones, and sang the progress to the entire company. We now had cheers and laughter where before there was fear and tedium.

Bob Nero was delighted with our new system and organized an open house for our shareholders' annual meeting so that they, too, could see the transformation. The sales team would bring visiting customers in for tours of "the factory."

My personal fire was burning brighter than ever. I couldn't wait to get to work now. No more late arrivals to work by long, slow, winding drives along country roads. James and I would stay late, making sure everything was ready for every stage of the biweekly iterations of our new process. It was all falling into place.

A Little Red Wagon

One of the challenges in the new space was that the typical office paradigm no longer made sense. Sharing computers and shifting the programming pairs frequently meant you couldn't possibly have your own personal space anymore. This brought up the practical issue of "What do I do with my stuff?" when you had to move to a different table and computer every two weeks. Tim, my energized and funny senior developer, brought in a little red wagon, a Radio Flyer with wooden, slatted sides. Every two weeks, he loaded his personal belongings into the wagon and moved to his new paired workstation.

This kind of clever, comical, inspired innovation was happening in ways small and large everywhere in the Java Factory—and almost none of it was top-down. The energy of playfulness lowered guards and trust began to build. I could hear it in the team's conversations. There was less *I* and a lot more *we*. Suddenly, when someone was in trouble or stuck, help arrived without even asking. If a pair was silently stuck at their computer, staring motionless at the screen, another pair would arrive and ask, "What's going on?" It felt safe and nurturing, rather than competitive and tense.

The Risk of Staying the Same

Within months of adopting our new approach, Interface Systems, Inc. had become the number one public company in Michigan based on stock growth. Our stock went from $2 a share to $80 a share. (Repeat after me: the Internet bubble. It was exciting, but it wasn't real.)

In the midst of this skyrocketing progress, one of my longtime programmers, David, approached me. "Rich, you had no idea this was going to work out this well. Why were you willing to take the risk on such a dramatic change?" he asked. "You had everything: the VP title, the position, the perch, the power, the pay, the stock options, the authority."

"It was actually quite easy," I said. The risk of staying the same had been far greater than the risk of change. My job hadn't been at risk, nor had my position or compensation. *I* had been at risk. The part of me that loved what I did and loved going to work had been dying. What was I going to do for the rest of my career if I couldn't do the thing that I so loved when I was a kid?

Around this time, a Silicon Valley suitor came along to evaluate Interface Systems for an acquisition. The due diligence team evaluated my team, our process, and our products. On September 1, 2000, it bought Interface at ten times the stock value from when I had decided to build the best damn software team this town had ever seen. To this day, Bob Nero credits my team's transformation as the primary reason for the successful sale of the company. We all felt like heroes and, on paper, we were, briefly, wealthy heroes.

But by early 2001, the Internet bubble had burst and our new California parent shuttered every remote office it had, including ours. The beautiful, high-flying experiment we'd run was over. And for the first time in a thirty-year technical career that had started in 1971, I was out of work.

Four of us—James Goebel and I, plus two of James's Appnet colleagues, Bob Simms and Tom Meloche—immediately began discussing forming a new company. We knew how to build a great engine room with a great and joyful culture. Sadly, the first one we had built was inside the *Titanic*. When the *Titanic* hit the iceberg, a perfectly good engine room went to the bottom. It wasn't the engine room's fault.

So we did it again. On June 12, 2001, Menlo Innovations LLC was born. At the beginning, there were just a few of us, five or six in all, as we worked to land projects at a time when our entire industry was collapsing around us. Many considered us crazy for starting an IT services company at the depth of our industry's depression. To the world, we appeared strangely confident—they didn't know what we knew.

We decided that our company's purpose would be to bring our joy to the world through the software we would design and develop for others, and to teach others about the joyful practices and systems we had conceived. It was never our plan to keep our approach

a secret. We had discovered something too fundamentally important to our industry to keep it to ourselves.

Lasting Joy

I am happy to say my personal flame is now burning brighter than
it ever has. My kids are now convinced I will never retire. They are
certain that one day a lifeless but smiling old man will be carried
out of the place that brought joy to himself, his business partners,
his team, and now the world.

The joy I've found is what I hope to reveal in our conversation
through this book. I don't assume what worked for me will work for
you, but I do want to inspire you as you contemplate what an intentional culture of joy could look like in your world. There will be
very real, sometimes painful stories and many examples of things
we have tried to make our world better, so you can experiment
along with us as you continue your search for joy in the workplace.

TWO

Space and Noise

First we shape our buildings, then they shape us.

—WINSTON CHURCHILL, 1943

L ate one summer afternoon, I had a meeting at a potential client's office. I waited in the lobby area while the receptionist let the CEO know I was there. From where I sat, I looked into the company's office space. High cube walls, standard-height drop ceiling, sterile, bright fluorescent light, and not a single item hung on the painted off-white walls.

Then I heard it—or rather, didn't. Library quiet. My ears were ringing from the deafening silence. It was late afternoon, so I simply assumed everyone was gone for the day.

The CEO came to retrieve me and ushered me back to her corner office. Together, we walked through a farm of a few dozen cubicles, all perfect replicas of one another. Every cube had a person in it, working very quietly. The space was bland, and I got the sense that the employees' work, owing to their surroundings, was likely to be uninspired. That office had no energy, no noise, and very likely no innovation. This was the polar opposite of Menlo.

Most workplaces zap energy because they are bland, prefabricated setups. These spaces diminish interactions with their physical barriers and closed doors. Creativity is further stifled by modern office furnishings that are not adaptable to changing needs. In every way, they are made to be quiet and lifeless. This is true even of the zany spaces of award-winning companies. Prize-worthy spaces are often built to win awards, not foster teamwork and energy. If you visit such companies, note how their work space is being used. Do the special features look brand new, even after years of being there? Is the space productive or simply beautifully designed?

Menlo's joy starts with our physical surroundings. We are set in a big, open "factory," full of chatter and activity. As you pull open the tall glass doors and walk in, you *feel* the energy of the place—it's palpable. You see an open space flooded with light. You see people working together. You hear laughter. Even the walls grab your attention as they are covered with papers and colorful posters. Our software factory might remind you of a popular, noisy, casually fun restaurant.

An organization of joy should be identifiable from every angle. You can't just tell people that you've built your company on the concept of joy in business—they need to see it and hear it for themselves from the first moment they encounter your space.

Tear Down the Walls

Menlo focuses on space that energizes. Our four office locations to date have all been wide open. In 2012, we moved into a seventeen-thousand-square-foot space in the basement of a parking structure in downtown Ann Arbor. This former food court had sat empty and dungeonlike for years before our renovations. Our office—or "factory," as we like to call it—has no walls, offices, cubes, or doors (with the few obvious exceptions for physical security and bathroom privacy). In our latest move, we added three glass-walled conference rooms because we've discovered that our clients aren't as used to our noise as we are. Ceiling heights in our space vary; some are twenty or thirty feet above us. Since the basement space has no windows, we put in lots of lights. Everyone is within eyeshot of one another, purposely, as we have tried to eliminate any barriers to simple human communication.

Our work surfaces consist of dozens of lightweight, five-foot aluminum tables with one computer on each. The tables are pushed close together, and the people working at them—two to a computer—sit even closer. Retractable electrical and wired network pull-down cables that hang from the high ceilings provide power and network connections.

The floor is concrete, polished and sealed, because we are messy and it's easy to clean. We host dogs at our office, which makes sealed concrete especially practical. Babies are also welcome, so there is often a Pack 'n Play set in the middle of the floor—not a typical office accessory, I'll grant you. These design aspects make our culture explicitly clear from the moment you walk in our doors.

Our walls are covered with colorful yarn and papers with sticky dots pushpinned to the wall. We've got plastic Viking helmets on tables, toys, and a disco ball hanging from the ceiling. There are posters pinned high on the walls, and we have an old plaster bust of Thomas Edison along with a working replica lightbulb to remind us of his lab in Menlo Park, New Jersey. Our three conference rooms are walled off by clear floor-to-ceiling glass and heavy, clear-glass sliding barn doors.

Drawing "Mobile" Inspiration from Fiction

One of my favorite television shows growing up was *M*A*S*H*, starring Alan Alda. Menlo has a lot in common with the Mobile Army Surgical Hospital and the 4077th unit, which had an amazingly competent yet playful culture.

I always found it fascinating that the unit itself was mobile. When the front lines moved during the Korean War, they could change their space and location quickly, even overnight if necessary. Likewise at Menlo, we have a space that is very flexible and made of lightweight mobile equipment. Three times in our history we have "bugged out" and moved to bigger space in a different part of Ann Arbor. Each time, we broke down our entire factory (tables, chairs, boards, computers, books—everything) on a Saturday and put it all back together in the new space on Sunday. By Monday morning, Menlonians were back at work, never having missed a workday on account of a move.

M*A*S*H taught me that playfulness helped relieve the tension of being in a war zone. Practical jokes, whimsy, and lack of respect for traditional authority of corporate culture keeps us energized and engaged. These qualities are amplified when you're in an open, flexible, mobile space. But what I perhaps most appreciated about *M*A*S*H* 4077th was that, when they were at work in the operating room, there was no question they were the best in the world at what they did. Although they could be irreverent and goofy, they were also serious and skilled. While the *M*A*S*H* workers didn't appreciate the human destruction that war had sent into their little mobile hospital, they were going to give everything they had to put injured humanity back together.

At Menlo, there is a similar, almost incomprehensible focus on the work, given the paradoxically playful surroundings. While we have many untraditional gadgets and furniture in our space, guests have reported in later retellings that they saw Ping-Pong and Foosball tables—things that aren't even there. Once you realize how many possibilities our space has, some visitors can't help but fill in blanks in their own heads. It is such high energy that occasional visitors—even those just stumbling upon our office—can sense it. I recall one package delivery person remarking immediately upon entering, "I don't know what you do, but whatever it is, I want to *work* here."

Menlo's wide-open, bright work space.

We Don't Need Space Police

We rearrange our factory often—weekly, sometimes daily. The well-placed wiring and the lightweight tables allow anyone on the team to change the space whenever the need arises. Menlo has no facilities people, and no permission is needed to make a change. The team can change the space whenever they like, in whatever configuration they want. Although I doubt it would happen at Menlo, our team could arrange themselves into a cube farm–like setting if they wanted.

Changing the layout typically occurs for two reasons. The first is out of necessity: if a new project starts or an existing one is expanded, the tables are rearranged to accommodate the new work. Our team wants everyone on the same project working next to one another. The programmers and High-Tech Anthropologists grab the tables and computers they need and push them together. Such a change occurs without any fanfare and usually takes only a few minutes—just enough time to push tables together and get the computers hooked up again.

The second reason for rearranging is change for the sake of change. If projects have been in the same part of the factory for too many weeks, the team grabs a twelve-pack of beer on a Friday evening and spends a few hours rearranging tables and computers just to shake things up. By changing their part of the factory real estate, they change their vantage point. This reenergizes everyone and builds our mental capacity for flexibility, as we all must get used to our new locations. Team members feel ownership of the whole space, not just their project's slice of it.

In one my favorite versions of "change the space," nothing actually moved. The first December in our newest space, a few team members banded together one weekend and painted a full winter scene—complete with elves, snowmen, a Christmas tree, and the word *JOY*—on the twenty-foot glass wall near our entrance. No one asked permission and no one confessed to being the artist. It was a clever and whimsical setup for our annual party.

The team sees every pillar and wall in our space as a blank canvas, to be adorned for practicality or whimsy. It also lets us say, The space is ours; we feel ownership and commitment to making it what we desire.

Our joyful holiday mural.

Where's the C-Suite?

Some may wonder where, in a wide-open, no-rules space, the CEO sits. Most companies mark the status of their high-level managers by gifting them suites. But our C-suite isn't a corner office; it's a table out in the middle of the space, with an old white Apple iMac, notable because it may be the slowest computer in the entire company. That's where I, as the CEO, sit.

Leaders at Menlo are not stuck on the traditional trappings of a corner office or the power statement of the biggest desk. My five-foot aluminum table is the same as the rest of the team's. I don't have the best or newest computer setup in the office, either. It's not that I want a slow old computer, but I don't *need* anything more modern. The fastest machines should be there for the team members who need such computing power to do their jobs. As CEO, I'm not programming; I research online, write documents, and check e-mail. I sit out in the middle of the room because that's where the team has put me.

Sometimes the team decides I need to be closer to the action, where I can overhear more of the details of a particularly challenging project. When that is the case, they move my table right into the mix of that project's pod of tables and people. Every few months I have to adjust my walking pattern to a new desk location.

Where Do We Go for Big-Dog Discussions?

In a space like ours, there are no big dogs. We hold most of our conversations where we sit because I want my team members to hear my client interactions. They care about our customers as much as I do, and they might have important data to add to the discussion.

Some might consider this eavesdropping. I consider it the simple, healthy curiosity of a team focused on the same goal. Most of my conversations are related to future work for the company they love and that puts food on the table. In most companies, clients are ushered through a cube farm to a closed-door conference room where big decisions are made in private. These closed meeting rooms send a powerful message: if you're on the wrong side of the door, you don't have the authority to participate in this discussion. It says, "You don't matter as much as I do." Menlonians should not feel left out of these conversations.

Quiet, Please, People at Work!

I am often invited to corporate environments around the country to speculate with company leaders about how to improve their respective team's energy and productivity. They lead me through the area where their technical team works. As we traverse the darkened sea of cubes, the conversation starts with the slightest whisper: "Rich, this is where our technical team works." Everyone sits in silence, with his or her back to the door, earbuds in place, monitor turned away from peeping eyes.

When we return to the CIO, CTO, or VP's spacious office, he closes the door and describes the communication challenges that are confronting his team. These high-level managers start describing all the fancy electronic collaboration tools they have installed for team members—most of whom sit five feet apart, separated by a thin cube wall and a vast distrust engendered by electronic-only relationships. Yet no one is actually *talking* to anyone else. When tone, inflection, and body language are missing from the conversation, there is little opportunity to build trust.

The software industry, especially, has a history of magnifying introversion with sensory deprivation cubicles and private offices. This isolation leads to solitary confinement, loneliness, and a feeling of loss of the support of their peers. Humans crave interpersonal contact and rely on nonverbal cues much more than formal language. A space like ours encourages human interaction in its many forms.

Joy Is Noisy

The Menlo Software Factory is alive with the hum of conversations and laughter. You can *hear* work. Our noise is just as notable as our space.

In *Working at Inventing: Thomas A. Edison and the Menlo Park Experience*, William Pretzer describes a similar environment at our namesake work space, Edison's Menlo Park lab. "Far from being sedate intellectual environments characterized by library quiet," he writes, "Edison's labs were noisy, crowded places that often seemed on the point of uproar."

In many industries it's a popular belief that silence is critical to establishing "flow," that state of optimal work. Even in the most sedate offices, though, it's never actually library quiet. In these environments, almost every worker has on headphones, listening to music or white noise. This itself offers direct evidence that "flow" does not require library quiet.

At Menlo, though, our "flow" is different. Our flow is team flow, not personal flow. We work noisily with one another. One of our few rules is that we ban earbuds. If you need earbuds to get into your state of flow, you're not the right fit for Menlo.

Critics say that a noisy environment like ours doesn't work. They declare that concentration is impossible. They believe nothing will get done. They forget about the annoying colleague three cubes away who talks loudly on his cell phone about last weekend's game. They don't remember the social butterfly next door who has everyone in the company stopping by for a coffee klatch. This drives them crazy and would drive me crazy, too. We don't have that at Menlo. The conversations you hear are about problem solving or design challenges. A respectful underlying current of useful noise is quite easy to handle. The noise you hear in our office is the noise of *work*.

Most modern business projects are complex endeavors that require teams working together in tight collaboration. Noise and its energy breed collaboration and teamwork.

Noise Creates Opportunity

A culture that embraces and honors its people with a changeable space encourages serendipity. The base element of serendipity in our lab, as in Edison's, is quite simply people overhearing others' ideas. Bumping into people and getting into unexpected conversations creates opportunities for regular and systematic innovations. This may be the single greatest value of a wide-open space.

If everyone is tired and stressed, and also allowed to close his or her door or block out the world with earbuds, the chances of overhearing others' ideas just won't occur. You will lose the majority of your opportunities for the innovative spark that leads to new ideas and approaches.

Don't ignore the opportunity to take big risks with physical setup and the auditory atmosphere. Space and noise play a huge factor in creating the opportunity for allowing teamwork to work its magic. Space and noise can also set you up for a powerful competitive advantage: a team that can learn faster than your competition.

Freedom to Learn

In the long run, the only sustainable source of competitive advantage is your organization's ability to learn faster than your competition.

—PETER SENGE, *The Fifth Discipline*

In 2010, I was at a technical conference in Salt Lake City with one of our senior programmers, Kealy, where we were to present our experiences with paired work. Programmers from companies around the nation were there. At lunch, she and I shared a table with a few of them.

Kealy started with Menlo right out of college in 2004. She knows only our style, although she's heard plenty of horror stories about our industry. At lunch, Kealy overheard several programmers introducing themselves to one another. One was a Java developer, another was a Microsoft .NET expert, still another programmed in Ruby. Kealy softly remarked to me how weird their exchange was.

The programmers overheard and wanted to know what she found so strange. She respectfully offered that she thought it was strange that they defined themselves by a piece of technology. They asked what kind of programmer she was. I'm a software programmer, she replied. They pushed her further. What language did she use—Java, C#, Ruby, .NET? She answered that she used whatever language worked best for the problem we were trying to solve. Exasperated, they asked where her technical allegiance lay. This was an easy answer for Kealy: with the technology that worked best for our customer. More than slightly annoyed, the programmers shrugged and went back to their conversation. They just didn't get why she didn't identify herself with the technology she knew or liked best.

Imagine how unprepared these programmers were when iPhones and the App Store were released a couple of years earlier. Suddenly a language called Objective-C became one of the most important programming languages on the planet. How did their language allegiance serve them in this brand-new world?

Our industry, like so many others, is subdivided into areas of expertise that require very specific knowledge. In medicine, where once general practitioners dominated, now we have radiologic urologic oncologists who specialize in X-ray treatment of prostate cancers at very specific stages. The world certainly benefits from specialists, but unfortunately what happens in so many specialty practices is that the solution almost always fits the specialty, no matter the problem. Very few specialists have the capacity or the interest to step back and take a broader view.

At Menlo, we don't limit ourselves to specific technical knowledge. Our software developers have experience in a variety of programming languages and readily choose the best technology for a given problem without being biased toward or needlessly faithful to a certain technology. This confounds most in our industry.

That's why we were able to adjust quickly to the language change brought by iPhones and the App Store. Our team went out and bought a book about Objective-C. Just days later, one pair of our programmers started building an iPhone app at the request of one of our clients. And no, the two weren't as fast on that project as they were with more familiar programming languages. But collaborative, on-the-fly learning is the basis of our competitive advantage. Through pairing, we give our team permission to learn.

Two Heads, Two Hearts, Four Hands,
One Computer

Pairing is the foundation of our work style and our learning system. Two people sit together at one computer, working all day on the same task at the same time. They share the keyboard and the mouse if they're programmers (or crayons and markers if they are High-Tech Anthropologists—more on that in chapter six). These pairs are assigned by our project management team and switch every week. While team members can advocate for a certain partner, one of our goals is to ensure that everyone gets a chance to work with everyone else.

In my earliest moments of contemplating paired work in the Java Factory at Interface Systems, I had to fight every one of my managerial instincts. This was an incredibly inefficient way to organize humans, right? Isn't it more productive to have each person work separately? Aren't we paying two people to do one job? What I have learned is that pairing is one of the most potent managerial tools I have ever discovered because of all the traditional problems it helps solve. Pairing fosters a learning system, builds relationships, eliminates towers of knowledge, simplifies onboarding of new people, and flushes out performance issues.

In the paired environment of Menlo, we are continuously building our skills. Each pair partner brings his or her own unique experience and knowledge to the conversation. When pairs work together, they often learn something new about their pair partner's unique breadth of experience. In most organizations, knowledge of a team member is first created by a résumé and then narrowly focused by that person's work experience and the distant understanding of his or her capabilities. There is typically no opportunity to discover hidden talents among existing team members.

I once paired with one of our programmers to prepare for a team presentation about storytelling. As this was the first time we worked together, I asked him about his life experience. In that brief conversation, I learned that he once worked for a leading voice recognition software company. What a coincidence—we had a longtime client who could take advantage of his knowledge! He had no idea this background would be useful to us and likely would not have offered it up on his own. This casual exchange of information, unrelated to the task at hand, could one day be useful to our work. In environments where people work alone, this type of serendipity is lost.

Learning happens every minute of every day while actual work is being done. One person in the pair teaches her new partner what she learned the previous week. For example, one week High-Tech Anthropologist Michelle learns about how prosthetics fit and how to calibrate artificial feet for below-the-knee amputees. The next week she pairs with Laura and has to bring her up to speed on everything she's learned that is relevant to the prosthetics software we

Ten pairs working on a project at tables pulled close to one another.

are designing. By immediately teaching someone else the information she has just learned, Michelle enhances her own understanding of the topic. The pairs teach and question one another, expanding on one another's knowledge in the process. If we do this for a few weeks, changing the pairs every week, before we know it half of our team is filled with budding experts and supportive teachers.

Learning to Get Along

Assigning pairs and switching them each week helps avoid a variety of typical team ills that could interfere with learning outcomes. For example, it prevents team members from feeling alienated by another team member who may not have a particularly outgoing personality. It may not be a personality problem at all, just normal human shyness. We avoid cliques forming, as everyone gets a chance to work with one another.

We've found that people are more likely to engage in a casual, pop-up conversation with others whom they've previously paired with for forty hours. This time spent together dispels a lot of misconceptions about one's fellow teammates. Once you spend forty hours in conversation with another human being, you are going to get to know that person in a deeper way than a general impression could ever accomplish.

Working in pairs also provides an emotional safety net for our employees. As much as they are stretching the boundaries of what they know, they are also testing the edges of what is "safe" in a work environment. When a new technology or process or domain is introduced, there's always the prospect of fear creeping in, a natural human response to the unknown.

Imagine a six-year-old child on an unfamiliar walk near the edge of a deep, dark forest. The child will stand frozen and frightened, unable to move forward. But place an equally frightened six-year-old friend beside him and together they may confidently travel this unknown space together, hand in hand. Just like the buddy system we learned in childhood swim classes, pairing helps us move into the unknown with confidence and courage, comforted by the safety such a system provides.

Watch Productivity Rise

A few weeks after one of our programmers joined Menlo, straight out of college, she received a phone call at home from one of her upset friends. They lamented that she wasn't answering their texts and their instant messages at work the way other friends were.

"I can't," she said. "I'm working. I'd be letting my pair partner down."

Visitors sometimes ask us how we can absorb the loss of productivity that pairing represents. Of course, there *is* no real loss, but tremendous gains as learning goes faster. Stuck people are quickly unstuck when their partner suggests a different approach. Quality soars with four eagle eyes on the screen, and we achieve a superior result in a shorter amount of time. One company we competed with for years (and now partner with as a client) claimed that, during the competitive period, they outspent us ten to one. They ultimately threw in the towel because we just got more done in the same amount of time.

Working in pairs doesn't mean that one person gets to slack off while another is glued to the keyboard. People who have just joined us leave at the end of an eight-hour day looking quite exhausted. When I ask them how their day was, they often say that they had a great day . . . but they are *really tired*. It's not that they've logged more hours at their desks at Menlo—it's just that they probably never worked even close to eight productive hours in an eight-hour day.

Informal research suggests that programmers generally work only about four hours a day with all the meetings, the workflow interruptions, and the distractions of the computer itself. This became far worse when the Web came along, and worse still with smartphones. Our pace and focus shocks those not used to it. When our team is working, distractions fade away—they are really working. New hires get used to this intensity after two or three weeks. It takes some conditioning to work in a company with such high productivity during a working day.

Can We Really Afford All This Learning?

Potential clients often hesitate when I tell them that our team will be learning something new while working on their project. They tell us they don't want to pay my team to learn on their dime. Of course, I try to reassure them that most of the knowledge my team will be applying has been learned on someone else's dimes, quarters, and million-dollar bills. Yet many still insist we put only experts on their project. They want people who have a deep understanding of their industry or at least three years of experience in the technology they've chosen.

If this traditional thinking persists, we are likely not a good fit for the client. We believe that relying on deep expertise stifles innovation. We may need to learn a new programming language or software tool for a client's project; our organization is built to handle this. We don't miss a beat when learning opportunities arise. We buy a book, crack it open, start to work, and learn simultaneously.

One of our clients, a local book manufacturer, was shocked to see that, within weeks, our team had a deeper end-to-end understanding of his business than any individual employee had within his decades-old company. We have a well-developed curiosity that allows us to see things that experts can easily overlook. This is where our most serious learning occurs. We have gotten deep into the processes and protocols of organ transplant surgery, diesel motor diagnostics, flow cytometry for cancer and AIDS research, book manufacturing, truck transmission testing, and many, many others. Our inquisitiveness and openness to learn from others help us to learn our client domains quickly—usually to a greater depth than most could begin to imagine. Learning how to learn fast, and as a group, is where our organization shines.

Tear Down Towers of Knowledge

Back in 1997, when I was promoted to VP of R&D at Interface Systems, I was ceremoniously installed by the board members at my first official board meeting. At a break, one of the longtime board members grabbed me by both shoulders, looked me straight in the eye, and said, "Welcome aboard, Rich. How is Dave doing?"

"Dave"—not his real name—was my key tower of knowledge, the person on my team who had vast technical knowledge that no one else had. That the board member knew his name sent me a clear message: keep Dave happy. The company's value, and therefore your job, depends on it. *One programmer* was key to the worth of a company that in 1999 was valued at over $400 million. No wonder I used to lose sleep whenever Dave took a two-week vacation.

Lest you think that the tower of knowledge enjoys being the center of attention in this way, think again. What may start out feeling like job security eventually becomes a prison from which your Dave cannot escape. He becomes the bottleneck of the entire organization. Vacations are impossible to schedule as Dave is always on the critical path for current projects and on call for customer emergencies. When Dave does get to go on vacation, his laptop goes with him. Work stacks up while he is away; low-level emergencies await his return.

What if one day Dave starts to yearn for new challenges and opportunities and wishes to learn something new and exciting? All he sees are the plum assignments going to the new guys. Why would the company burden Dave with a project outside his comfort zone when he's so good at one thing? His comfy little tower starts to feel like a rusted bear trap clamped around his ankle, chaining him to the desk. Sadly, he can't even quit to escape his tower because of the way our industry hires. His résumé will show knowledge in only one particular space. Every company needs what Dave knows, and so he will just end up in the same tower in his new job. Until, of course, the industry no longer needs what he knows. Poor Dave. I hope his 401(k) is well funded.

In talks, I often ask the audience members if their company has a tower of knowledge on their team. The majority of those in the room usually raise their hands. I then ask them to share the first name of their tower of knowledge. Slowly, nervously, the first names start flowing. People *always* know the name of their tower. And if they don't, they just might be the tower of knowledge themselves.

Next, I ask if this "tower" buys lottery tickets. Quiet laughter usually follows. It's pretty obvious that, although they rely on their tower of knowledge heavily, they are fully aware that there's no guarantee that that tower will always work for their company.

I ask these same questions of executives I meet one-on-one. What if their Dave, the guy in sales with the sterling client relationships, won $10 million in next week's lottery? Would he come to work the next day? Most managers assure me that "Dave" loves working at their company, so it wouldn't be a problem. They firmly believe that $10 million couldn't keep Dave away from his desk.

During one such meeting with an executive of a health insurance provider, I was able to speak to a "Dave." I asked him what he would do if he won the lottery. He assured me he'd be back at work the next day . . . to collect his personal belongings, say good-bye to his friends, and ceremoniously toss his cell phone in the trash basket. Dave's boss was just a little shocked to hear this, but Dave wasn't afraid to share this disloyal thinking with me in front of the boss. After all, he couldn't be fired. He was way too important.

This style of team organization is prevalent in many industries and so commonly accepted that management refuses to acknowledge the risk of putting all its knowledge eggs in one brain basket. It would be as silly as a bank manager being the only one with the combination to the vault. But it's worse. At least bank vaults can be drilled open and the contents retrieved. When your tower of knowledge leaves, he takes too much with him that can't be re-created or taken back. There is often a desperate attempt to transfer decades of knowledge in the last two weeks of a tower's employ.

Imagine an airline where every plane was different enough that each pilot had to have unique knowledge to fly it. Perhaps one was an old DC-3, one was a helicopter, the next a glider, and still another a Boeing 747. If you lost the pilot, you lost the use of the plane, maybe forever. It may seem amusing or trite, but so many industries take just that type of risk, particularly those that create intellectual property or those that establish intricate practices based on the personal knowledge and experience of one individual.

Companies go to unbelievable extremes to protect and coddle their towers of knowledge. One company had such a serious problem with this scenario that they had *roped off* the software code of a part of their mission-critical system that only their Dave knew. Dave had taken another job and was no longer working for the company, but the rest of the team was instructed to never, ever change Dave's code. No one could make sense of Dave's code, and if someone broke it, no one would ever be able to figure out how to fix it.

I caught up with one of this company's executives a few years later and asked how it was going. Had they ever allowed people to work with Dave's code? Did they still prevent their current employees from touching this roped-off area? The executives were delighted to inform me that their problem had been solved: their Dave had returned to work for them. They got lucky. You can't assume that your Dave, would ever come back.

In a paired environment that switches the pairs regularly, this knowledge hoarding just isn't even a possibility. Pairing, by its nature, eliminates knowledge hoarding. We switch pairs weekly because doing so knocks down towers of knowledge each and every week. There is no one person on our team who is the only one to understand a piece of the system or the subtleties of a particular algorithm.

The benefit to the team members is also quite clear. In twelve years we've never had to deny a request for time off. Without towers of knowledge, our people are under pressure to perform well at work—but not because they're the only ones who can do a given job.

Pairing Pushes Personal Growth

We don't tolerate towers of knowledge or lone geniuses at Menlo, but that doesn't mean people can get away with not pulling their weight. Could you hide at Menlo by always being the student in a pair and be carried along each week by your peers without having to retain anything you've learned? No. At Menlo, the straggler—let's call him Danny—becomes known to everyone quickly, because we switch the pairs every week. If Danny can't teach a system he learned one week to a new partner the next, it becomes obvious very quickly. A team member who, every day, jumps on the two-man sled, looks at his pair partner, and says, "Pull me," does not last long, especially because, as you will learn later, hiring, firing, and promotion decisions are peer led. Good pair partners must be teachers as well as students.

The hidden benefit of giving your team members the freedom to learn is that, eventually, they will embrace the idea of taking the time to teach. Knowledge isn't kept away in secret personal vaults like the crown jewels of little kingdoms. The workers on your team become more valuable as they learn new practices; they also become more flexible. Some conclude that this diminishes each team member's unique value and turns each one into a cog in our little software factory machine. Usually, in the very next breath they tell us how amazingly valuable each of our team members is because of his or her mastery of so many different technologies and domains. This can happen only when you truly believe your team members are equally valuable and equally able to learn and carry certain knowledge.

Pairing is the atomic element of our learning organization. It produces a joy in learning that most of us haven't experienced in years, perhaps since elementary school, when everything was new and all we had to do was absorb it.

The Lunch 'n Learn

We are both teachers and students in a paired arrangement, but Menlo also offers other learning opportunities beyond the two-person team. At least once a week we host an organized "Lunch 'n Learn." This is a long-standing tradition, started back in the days of the Java Factory at Interface Systems. What we discovered back then is that important learning happens in the pairs rather quickly, but the knowledge transfer to the rest of the team can be slow. To facilitate team learning, we bring in lunch and grab a corner of the factory, typically at noon, to hold deeper teaching sessions. We rearrange tables, chairs, flip charts, and whiteboards on wheels and gather around that day's teachers. The Lunch 'n Learn most commonly deals with a topic directly related to the client work we are doing. This might involve a technology topic like Android development or a team exercise like brainstorming.

While Menlonians are teaching, they are also learning to present in front of groups and organizing materials in a compelling way. We want our team members to be good presenters and teachers who can speak at conferences (and represent Menlo). Our Lunch 'n Learn format gives them the opportunity to build self-confidence to present in front of others, with a safe and caring test crowd.

Menlonians also regularly offer to lead a Lunch 'n Learn on a subject they've taken a deep interest in. While the topics are typically related to some aspect of our business, we do have a wide range of interests. If someone on the team reads a good business book that she believes has lessons for the rest of us, for example, she will schedule a Lunch 'n Learn and teach us—one recent session presented the book *Rework*. When team members attend a conference, they come back and share their experience. For instance, Carol M. came back from a conference and taught us how to powerfully visualize a project's big picture using a technique called story mapping. One month's worth of Lunch 'n Learn postings on the office refrigerator included topics as varied as Improv, Design Tools, Storytelling, Sleuthing Workflows, Negotiation and Confrontation, and Drawing/Sketching.

Not all of our content comes from the team itself. Plenty of interesting experts from the community, such as professors from the University of Michigan, are willing to share their knowledge and experience with us. One of our more memorable lunchtime speakers was Dr. Jim Bagian, a doctor, professor, engineer, business process expert, and astronaut, who mesmerized the team with tales from the 337 hours of flight time he logged in space shuttle missions. He taught us about risk taking, and how he managed his own fear in pursuit of his version of joy. We Menlonians are not risking our lives during our job the way Jim did as a shuttle pilot, but his joyful desire to be part of something big taught us about mission, purpose, and sacrifice.

Our Lunch 'n Learns have also become community affairs. If someone outside the company catches wind of an interesting Lunch 'n Learn we are holding, we invite that person to attend. We share a glass wall with TechArb, the University of Michigan's student start-up incubator, and students there know they are free to confer with us whenever they feel the need. If a Lunch 'n Learn comes up on a technical topic such as unit testing for iPhone apps and we know some of those student teams are working on iPhone apps, we'll be sure to invite them. It's a good way to expand the base of people who know us and know our story. And you never know what value they might bring as well.

Teach the World Your Culture

Beyond Lunch 'n Learns, we believe in publicly offering formal classes about our process and culture. In the very early Menlo days, it was only James and I (and our former partner Tom) who did the teaching. Now James and I barely do any of the teaching. Our team members sign up to create and deliver the curriculum to clients who sign up for our paying classes. The students in these classes come from businesses and organizations around the world, including the Knight Foundation, Bose Corporation, General Motors, Medtronic, and many others.

Menlonians regularly teach all elements of our process to any willing learners, including our competitors. No part of our process is a trade secret. Our mission, which we take very seriously, is to "end human suffering in the world as it relates to technology." This doesn't just mean we're trying only to end our suffering or that we believe only Menlo-designed technologies can ease human suffering. We want everyone to have a better and more meaningful work life.

Regular classes we offer include the broad overview "The Menlo Way," our High-Tech Anthropology approach to design, our project management techniques, and our software development approach on finer subjects such as automated unit testing. We've also taught our unique style of brainstorming, usually in the context of helping the class attendees brainstorm a practical aspect of their business. Some of our clients desire a custom blend of our standard offerings, so we pull together a private class with customer content based on their needs. It's not unusual for us to earn 5 percent to 10 percent of our annual revenue just from teaching. It is not a central focus of our business model, but it is core to our mission.

Being an active learning organization strengthens our team and makes them more valuable to Menlo and to our clients. Sustaining and enhancing our ability to share our message with one another and with those outside the company is central to our culture. To reinforce our culture, just as any group of people does, we have rituals and artifacts.

Conversations, Rituals, and Artifacts

The most exciting breakthroughs of the 21st century will not occur because of technology but because of an expanding concept of what it means to be human.

—JOHN NAISBITT, *Megatrends*

My early career before Menlo consisted of mimicking my managerial mentors. I used to hold traditional status meetings every Monday morning at nine a.m. The team prepared status reports ahead of time and believed I would spend a good portion of my weekend reviewing the submitted material (which I rarely did). During the meeting, we sat around a big table in a conference room and went over everyone's highlights. All the usual questions came up: What did you accomplish last week? Are you ahead of or behind on your goals? What is your plan to make up lost ground?

This was not a productive conversation. I can assure you no one wanted to be there. Most team members were silent as their peers reported out. The only personal highlight for anyone attending the meeting was finding out if someone was further behind than he was, so that he could be assured someone else was on the critical path. If true, then the weekend wouldn't be ruined trying to catch up with everyone else.

One Monday morning, I was unexpectedly delayed at home by some important family issues and didn't get a chance to call in to tell the team I was going to be late for our meeting. When I came into work later that day, I asked whether the team had still met. "Well," they said, "*sort of.*" The team members had assembled in the conference room at nine a.m. and started chatting about their weekends while they waited for me to arrive. By about nine twenty-five, they realized I wasn't coming. Ten minutes later, they finally decided to go back to work. It took thirty-five minutes for that meeting to *not* begin.

This revealed an important truth: meetings like these are unnecessary. If you have meetings scheduled with your team, and they behave the way I've just described, then kill the meeting. My former team very clearly articulated that this meeting had no value for them. They were there only because the boss told them to be there.

At Menlo, we have eliminated unproductive, joyless meetings from our process. We have replaced rules, bureaucracy, and hierarchy with predictable rituals, ceremonies, and storytelling events. These have a clear structure, and there are clear expectations for every participant. Everyone knows the purpose of these gatherings, his or her individual responsibilities, and exactly how decisions are made and documented.

Typical corporate bureaucracy uses rules to limit the sharing of information and decision-making power. It establishes boundaries that cannot be crossed. Most of the organization concludes it is not allowed to participate, so it doesn't. While we still have a few strong rules that frame our rituals, storytelling, and artifacts, they are acceptable and honored because of our shared belief system. Our rules contribute to the human energy of our culture rather than steal from it.

The Daily Standup

In place of unproductive weekly status report meetings, we've instituted a daily standup ritual. Our daily standup occurs every day at ten a.m., regardless of who is in the room, and it goes the same way whether James and I are there or not. It almost always finishes in thirteen minutes or less, even if the group is as large as fifty or sixty people.

A dartboard alarm goes off at ten a.m. to signal that it's time for the daily standup. Everyone stands up and gathers in a rough circle to report out to the group. Someone grabs a Viking helmet to start the meeting. The pair partners holding the helmet describe what they are working on and where they might need help. The helmet is passed to the next pair in the circle, all the way around. The last pair closes with "Be careful out there." This ends the daily standup.

A seven-dollar plastic Viking helmet has become the iconic symbol of Menlo. In the spirit of *fun with a purpose*, we use this artifact because the two horns on the Viking helmet make it very easy for a pair to report out, each pair partner holding a horn. The helmet artifact serves a serious mission of providing order and structure to our standups, while also letting us maintain some level of irreverence. Yes, every once in a while someone puts on the helmet. I once donned it for a newspaper profile of Menlo.

The entire team gathered in a circle for the daily standup.

Rituals should reinforce cultural values. Our standup meeting is democratic and inclusive; everyone has an equal voice at this meeting. No one is *running* the meeting. It is intended to be valuable to everyone, not just management. Team members contribute as much or as little as they see fit. There is no requirement to contribute anything when it is your turn. On any given day, some have more to say than others. There is also a politeness factor at work that never seems to need a reminder: don't talk too long.

"Hey, Menlo!"

When we communicate with each other inside the company, we don't use e-mail or other forms of electronic communication. So many traditional office workers spend hours of their day checking e-mail, often quite unproductively. We've developed a far more efficient method of communication that we call High-Speed Voice Technology.

The hardware comes preinstalled: vocal cords, body language, tonal inflection, eyebrows, and facial expressions. Similarly, the receiver comes with tympanic membranes and cleverly designed auditory nerve stimulation of the brain.

To demonstrate this revolutionary communication technology to factory visitors, I pick out a Menlonian like Emily, one of our project managers, and say, "Hey, Emily!"

"Hey, Rich!" she instantly replies, making eye contact across the room. In this simple exchange, I have just demonstrated to our visitors how High-Speed Voice Technology can be used to have a meeting. Using my best manners, I thank her, and the meeting ends.

No one else moved or was interrupted by this exchange. Quite honestly, no one even heard it. The brain is an amazing filter. In particular, the reticular activator portion of the brain is excellent at allowing us to block out conversations we don't need to participate in. As a kid, I was always amazed that my dad could sit in his favorite living room chair, buried behind the evening paper, and not hear anything we were saying—until one of my older brothers mentioned plans for an upcoming road trip to Toledo with friends. "Where are you going and why?" Dad would ask while dropping the shield of his newspaper. Had he actually been listening to our conversation the whole time? Not a chance. As the old Simon and Garfunkel song says, "A man hears what he wants to hear and disregards the rest." That's your reticular activator at work.

Despite the almost comical simplicity of this "meeting" I held with Emily, it stands in stark contrast to the great difficulty in most organizations just to schedule time to talk. In "lean manufacturing" terminology, this is a great demonstration of eliminating the waste of excessive motion. I called the meeting, she attended, we communicated, and we were back to work in less than seven seconds. No conference room to book, no calendar synced, no endless e-mail circles to find a time that works for both of us. In fact, our meeting required no movement at all save a slight twist of the neck and long-distance eye lens refocusing.

In a culture that understands the utility of noise, it's nearly as easy to call an all-company meeting as it is a one-on-one. I just call out, "Hey, Menlo!"

"Hey, Rich!" the team responds in almost perfect unison. The entire office falls perfectly quiet in less than a couple of seconds. It's that simple to be in an all-company meeting with my team. Once we finish our discussion in a few minutes, I thank them (which ends the meeting), and everyone turns back to his or her work. We use this system, for example, to relay good news. I will typically call out, "Hey, Menlo!" when a new client deal is inked. The team cheers, perhaps asks a question or two, and then it's back to work. Throughout the day, you'll hear different versions of such impromptu meetings. There will be quieter callouts to individuals: "Hey, James!" for example. Or the team calls out, "Hey, Gobstopper!" to garner the attention of the team working on the Gobstopper project.

It's Not Just Noise, It's Constant Conversation

Pairing creates the most obvious and regular opportunity for systematic conversation. Pair partners have to learn to think out loud and how to be active listeners, because at Menlo conversation is a constant from the beginning to the end of the day.

As talking is a necessity in our paired environment, our space is filled with the noise of work. Noise energizes and creates openings for new conversations between pairs and across the room. In contrast, quiet work spaces tend to be self-reinforcing. Our manners suggest we should not bother people in a quiet environment. The typical cube farm simply magnifies the stereotypical social awkwardness of introversion, rather than capitalizing on its benefits.

Most visitors assume Menlo and paired work could work only for extroverts. While I am no expert in personality temperaments, when asked, the majority of our team self-identify as introverts. This makes sense to me for several reasons:

- Introversion supports the deep thinking needed to solve complex problems.
- Introverts prefer fewer, deeper relationships.
- Introverts are often better, active listeners.

Constant, mutual conversation works in our environment and contributes to our ability to work efficiently and make clear decisions.

Conversations Build Relationships, Relationships Build Value

These conversations help solve problems when they arise. When we use conversation as a building block for our meeting rituals, then we begin to really function as a team.

A great example of this comes from Zingerman's Roadhouse, a restaurant on the west side of Ann Arbor. Zingerman's is famous for its food, service, and culture. The restaurant holds weekly huddles, in which everyone from waitstaff to management meets for an hour to run the business together. During one of these sessions, the issue came up that the cost of goods sold was too high. The dishwasher pointed out the high volume of wasted French fries being tossed every day. He was in a unique position to watch the waste metrics for the business—after all, who would see waste more clearly than the dishwasher?

By opening their conversation up, the Zingerman's Roadhouse team came up with a solution that was beautiful and consistent with their abundance mentality. Cut the kitchen's per plate French fry quantity in half, thereby reducing cost of goods sold, and then offer free refills so as not to diminish customer value. Customers loved it, even though most never asked for a second helping. Waste plummeted.

Through sustained conversation, James and I see the chance to build deep relationships within our team, truly embrace change, and actually get meaningful things done. We want to work through difficult conversations together and point those conversations at *the issue* rather than at the people discussing the issue.

Conversations that feel as if we are both on the same side of the table working together toward a shared goal are critical to our relationship-building process. I recall a time when our automated unit testing framework, a critical part of our quality control practice, was taking well over thirty minutes to complete each time it was run for our largest client project. Our programmers were lamenting how debilitating this was, as these tests would bring certain processes to a standstill until completed. Our client wanted all our time spent on feature development, not improving a testing tool that doesn't even ship with the product.

I asked the team to outline how many hours of feature development were being lost each week by this slower unit testing process. Armed with this information, the client would be able to understand the impact of the performance problem on the thing they valued most: feature development. Once the work was expressed in terms the client could evaluate using their own priorities, it was easy to invite them into the conversation. At the time of this writing, more than twenty-six thousand unit tests are running in under ten minutes. We achieved this productive outcome once we facilitated a meaningful conversation between the business sponsor and the technical team.

If you can get two sides of your business (such as your business and production teams, or developers and clients) into regular and healthy conversations where it feels like a partnership, you can avoid the vicious war of competing values.

Making Room for Casual Conversation

Several years ago, our team decided that the stretch of time after lunch until the end of the day was quite exhausting without a break. They invented three o'clock "walkies," now a tradition. At three o'clock, Jeff J. calls out "Walkies!" in a deep, booming voice that has earned him the playful title of VP of High-Speed Voice Technology. If Jeff is not in that day, diminutive Lisa H. does an excellent imitation.

The team then stands, puts coats on if necessary, and walks around the building to stretch and take a break. I had imagined that this was their chance to get away from one another and talk about nonwork things of interest. While that probably happens, the one day I tagged along I saw that they stayed in their pairs and talked about the story card they were working on. This is yet another example of casual but supportive and constructive conversation.

Rituals Provide a Safe Environment for Building Skills

One of the most useful assets in any industry is the ability to communicate complex ideas to other people. Yet how many times do we ever get to practice this skill before we need to present for real in front of a group of people we don't know? It is little wonder that most people fear public speaking more than death.

Our rituals ensure that all team members, at one time or another, will present in front of a group. It would be easy to simply rely on the same people every time, or always pick the most seasoned and polished presenters, but we switch it around so everyone has a chance to practice. Menlonians present to one another in weekly kickoff meetings and to customers at weekly Show & Tells; they present at local conferences on subjects of interest to them and the audience; they lead tours of our factory. We even host local chapters of Toastmasters every now and then.

Our rituals also encourage healthy debate. When creating something new and innovative, there is no clear path to the desired outcome. Every person will have a different thought about potential solutions. Spirited team debate and respectful arguing produce better outcomes. We practice this kind of debate all day long. Each pair will have small arguments about competing approaches. Sometimes a debate will escalate (in a controlled manner) to include more pairs and a whiteboard. Most organizations revert to debate by proxy, often via e-mail. In the worst-case scenario, these e-mail morph into passive-aggressive conversations in which the argument doesn't actually ever play out. The software created in such an environment often doesn't work at all, because the competing factions on the team could never agree on the big picture—all the little pieces worked; they just didn't work together. One of the key elements of a joyful culture is having team members who trust one another enough to argue.

Estimation: Predicting the Future

Organizations need to predict the future. How much revenue will we have next quarter? How many cars will we sell? How many new deals will we close by February? How long will it take to build this bridge and how much will it cost? Much of this revolves around estimating, which is another word for "our best guess using limited information."

Typically, estimation is a job for management. Once a team has evaluated a project, management dictates how long the team has to complete an assignment, how much it can spend, or how much it must sell next quarter. There may be some lip service given to asking the team what it thinks, but mostly a team's attempt to estimate is seen as sandbagging.

At Menlo, all estimates come from the team that will actually be doing the work. Our estimation ritual is an open-book discussion conducted once a week in a group setting. The project manager prepares the necessary information and schedules the project team discussion. Each pair assigned to the project this week receives a packet of photocopied story cards and an estimation sheet that breaks down the project by hours needed to work on it. The project manager reads off a card, and each pair at the table discusses and circles an estimate choice on the sheet. The only choices it has are two, four, eight, sixteen, thirty-two, or sixty-four hours for any given estimate sheet.

With an estimate, we are simply seeking a good guess. If, while discussing, the pair partners think another pair would have a better idea, they are free to ask them for input, using High-Speed Voice Technology. As everyone doing this estimation is sitting around the same table, they can all hear the question and the answer.

Estimation is one of our most important conversations, as the team goes over every potential task for the coming week. At the end of this ritual, the project manager receives the estimation sheets from every pair. Each story card will have several estimates. It is not our goal to get everyone to agree on the estimate, as we accept that different pairs will have different reasons for varying estimates. Experience, skills, familiarity can all affect an estimate. But in this practice, the entire team has a chance to grasp the bigger picture, not just the tasks that will be assigned to its individual members.

Our quality advocates are a part of the estimation ritual as well. Why is this important? Most quality teams are brought in well after development is finished and they have little idea where the product's pitfalls lie. Some may think this keeps their bias pure, but in fact the quality team needs to hear where the concerns are in the code while the code is being developed. By involving QA in the estimation ritual, it hears the team describing a section of code that will be difficult to change in order to accommodate the task on the story card. The quality team can ask questions that will inform its testing strategies for the coming week. If its members sense confusion about a story card during estimating, they can ask simple questions like,

"How will QA be able to determine if this card is done?" If the answer raises too much confusion, the card will be rewritten before the work starts.

Every organization has to predict the future based on incomplete information. By doing this as a group while thinking out loud with one another, our estimation process creates safety and reduces fear of the unknown. This practice also builds our capacity for sizing new projects. Because we practice estimating every week, the team is seldom fazed by diving into new domains.

Show & Tell: Where Rubber Meets Road

In the broad world of work, any work being done by a team has a sponsor. That sponsor is not directly involved in doing the work; rather, sponsors are authorizing the work and, in most cases, paying for it.

At home, for example, if a room needs to be painted, you may choose to hire a painter. In this scenario, you are sponsoring the project but the painter is doing the work. And even if you decide to do the painting yourself, the sponsor may still be someone else. If I paint my daughter's bedroom, my wife is typically the sponsor, and my daughter will be the end user of the painted room.

The sponsor has an idea in mind as to what the outcome of the work will be. In the example above, the sponsor can picture in her mind what the painted room will look like. But the painter also has a picture of the outcome. Hopefully, the two pictures match, but sometimes they don't. Words and paint samples don't work as well as actually seeing the room itself painted. I have no idea what the difference is between off-white and China white when my wife is describing the color she wants.

At Menlo, we resolve these two competing mental pictures in a weekly ritual with our clients that we call Show & Tell. In Show & Tell, the team that worked on the project for the past week sits and watches while our client explains *our* work to *us*. If Ted and Rob worked on building a Web site form for submitting a book for printing, the client representatives from the book manufacturer will review the work by sitting together at a computer, navigating the Web site, and presenting their findings *back* to Ted and Rob and anyone else associated with that project. This makes perfectly clear what each side understands of the work that has been done and clarifies whether or not the sponsor and team are of one mind. We reverse the traditional Show & Tell process to ensure that our customer is actively engaged in the conversation, while our team watches, listens, and gives feedback to questions asked by the client.

One of our more fascinating Show & Tells occurred in the very beginning of our work on the software for the Accuri flow cytometer, which is a complex medical research tool that examines cells by exciting them with a laser and capturing the data represented by the laser light scatter that bounces off the cells. One of our very first tasks was to create a simple application with three buttons for ON, OFF, and EXIT. When the user clicked ON with the mouse, a single green LED on a prototype circuit board would light up. Clicking OFF would shut off the light, and EXIT quit the program.

Jennifer, the Accuri CEO and project sponsor, came in for Show & Tell. She talked our team through the program and showed us our work. The system worked as planned: ON, OFF, ON, OFF, again and again. No big deal, really, except that Jen jumped out of her seat, cheering, and promised to show the result at her next board meeting. Our team was confused by this reaction to such a simple outcome.

Jen's delight seemed out of proportion to the effort and complexity required for this task. But, as she explained, the obvious completion of this simple task demonstrated huge progress. "I have been doing this kind of thing for a long time," Jen said, "and you have just demonstrated that my hardware team and my software team are actually communicating, just two weeks into the project. That's huge! Most companies don't get confirmation of such cross-team collaboration until months or years into device development."

Show & Tell is a critical interaction. The client gets to discuss the project with the people who actually did the work. The people who did the work can hear and see the client's emotion in response. Sometimes the client is thrilled, other times simply ho-hum, and then, at times, frustrated or disappointed. We want the team to see and feel the full range of emotions, rather than have it described to them later in a managerial interpretive dance. The entire team of people who worked on that project this week get to see how their piece of the work fits together with the work of others on the project. If there is a disconnect in any way between what was planned and what actually happened, it is openly discussed right then and there by the people directly connected with the work.

Sometimes a client will say, "Oh, is that what you thought we meant?" At other times we get, "Oh, that's exactly what I asked for, but now that I see it, I realize it's not actually what we need." We consider both of these outcomes fine, since they're in line with *making mistakes faster*, one of our founding philosophies. If we make mistakes fast and discover them early, then we have a chance to correct them while they are still small and while there is still time and budget left to make changes.

Human communication is fraught with the perils of misunderstanding, miscommunication, and unstated assumptions. These perils are the foundational basis of most relationship problems. What one side sees as obvious, the other can't even comprehend. For us, the only way to knock down this wall of misunderstanding is to get the players together and put them in a structured ritual that involves touching and seeing the technology under development.

Planning Game: Forcing Hard Choices

Most business projects begin in a way reminiscent of a boat launch, where the mooring ropes have simply been lifted off and everyone waits and watches as the waves start lapping and the boat drifts, slowly and unceremoniously, away from shore. In most launches, you've set the budgets, established the time frames, and determined the team size and composition. Next come the burning questions: Where do you begin? What is the plan? How will the work be organized by the individuals doing the work?

Like an unceremonious boat launch, starting projects is often a challenge for most companies, but keeping them properly directed after launch is even more challenging. Most projects drift into a sea of ambiguity as sponsors lose track of the work's progress and the team has trouble keeping everyone informed and involved. This widening information disconnect sends the boat on a direct course for the rocky shoals of lost executive sponsorship. Once executive sponsorship is lost, the project will crash and sink.

At Menlo, we steer a project's direction with our client using a weekly planning game. Using the "Planning Origami" technique (which we'll see in greater detail in chapter seven), project managers guide our client through the effort of placing folded paper story cards on planning sheets that physically represent both time and budget. The folded story cards represent the features and time estimates as determined in the earlier estimation ritual, and the planning sheets represent the amount of time available each week.

This simple exercise facilitates the most important conversations and decisions that a client can make to keep its project on course. A typical project isn't steered by a single individual. R&D has one set of top priorities, executive management another set, and marketing, sales, and customer support still others. All of these competing priorities must be resolved with one another so that the highest and most sensible priorities are worked out in a group discussion.

Working on a planning game by fitting in task cards on a sheet of paper that corresponds to actual work hours.

In this weekly conversation, the basic questions of project management must be worked through without ambiguity. What's in and what's out? What comes first? What is next? What fits into the plan this week? What can wait? What can't? Is there a less expensive alternative to implement this feature? Is anything missing? Do we really need this? All of these points and more will be discussed between the client's project sponsor and our project manager. Often the sponsor will bring others along with him to represent the competing voices within their own company. By the time planning is done, the priorities are set. It is clear to all. Either the folded cards are on the planning sheets and thus authorized to be worked on or they are not on the planning sheets and will not be worked on. It is that clear and simple.

The planning game is a weekly discussion, and it isn't always easy, but our simple planning ritual forces the conversation. No project team ever has the luxury of waiting for perfect information. However, we still need to make decisions. It is better that those decisions be made in the course of a collaborative conversation and ritual rather than in an empty office late at night by some tired project manager futzing around all alone.

The Work Authorization Board: Freedom Through Tyranny

Once the planning game is completed, a project manager assigns one week of selected story cards to individual pairs assigned to that project. This is done neither verbally nor with e-mail, but rather with one of the most celebrated artifacts in our space: the Work Authorization Board.

Team members looking at the Work Authorization Board. It's very clear to anyone who examines this artifact which team members are responsible for what task on any given day, for any given project.

These visual displays are obvious to even the casual visitor because they look quite orderly and are ubiquitous in our space. Every different project has its own Work Authorization Board, made up of a rectangular matrix of story cards pushpinned to the Homasote walls. Each column of a project's matrix of cards represents a pair of people assigned to work together and the cards assigned to that pair for the next five days. Each row represents a day of the week. The pair's names are listed on a title card at the top of their column.

The beautiful part of this granddaddy of Menlo visual displays is that there is no ambiguity. Each pair knows which project it is assigned to this week and what its work plan is for the next five days. It is complete and total tyranny. This may be a funny statement for one of the world's most democratic companies, I know. But this is where the freedom of our culture really kicks in. The pair partners can pursue the work that they love without someone hanging over their shoulder asking, "How's it going? Whatcha working on?" We don't need that guy.

Each pair has a rational amount of work, based on its own estimates. The pair partners work on tasks sequentially, from top to bottom, focusing on exactly one card at a time until they get stuck or they finish. Either way, the partners move to the next card in their lane. If they run out of cards early, they help another pair by signing up to take a card in another lane. If everyone is caught up, they can move on to the "pull-ahead" cards, which are stacked and pushpinned under a separate index card and represent the forthcoming priorities selected by the client during planning. This keeps everyone on task all week on the sponsor's highest priorities.

Don't believe for a minute that this system can apply only to software teams. Some Menlo parents have used this same system to organize their kids' chores on the refrigerator. Jeff Schox, a patent attorney in San Francisco, uses a version of this board to organize his team's work. You will find similar systems in place at manufacturing firms, even those as large as Toyota.

Sticky Dots: A Real-Time Status Report

What if you could instantly tell a project's status at any moment day or night, without having to call a meeting or even talk to anyone? Sound unlikely? Not at Menlo. After thirty seconds of explanation, even visitors can report the status of a Menlo project, identifying which pairs are ahead, which pairs are behind, and the overall performance of a project team in relation to this week's schedule. The observant person—without having to interact with the people doing the work—can even detect which pairs are having more difficulty on their story card than others. Colorful sticky dots tell the story.

Each individual story card worked on at Menlo has its own structured life cycle. As pair partners begin work on a story card, they put a yellow sticky dot on the card under their names on the wall to signify that they've started the paired effort. When the pair *thinks* they are done, they ask our High-Tech Anthropologists for a quick check to see whether the newly completed work supports what was written on the card.

If everything looks okay, the card is labeled with an orange dot to signify "We think we are done." The orange dot is a signal to our quality advocates that the work on the card needs checking. The QA pair will talk with the programming pair who worked on the card, and the four of them review the completed work in what amounts to a mini Show & Tell. If the QA check is completed and satisfactory, the team can now move forward, knowing that the work on the card is complete.

The critical conversation between the team doing the work on the card and the pair of quality advocates checking the work is a fascinating collaboration. There is likely to be disagreement and perhaps even argument. However, they all know the real goal is to produce the best possible result for the upcoming client Show & Tell.

In contrast to my old life, when the QA team usually began checking programmer work months after the code was originally completed, Menlo's quality advocates sit right with the programming team and enjoy the exact same pay scale as our programmers. They get to sit in and participate in every conversation described above. Once they give the go-ahead on a given card, the work continues.

A "completed card" is labeled with a green dot placed over the orange dot. If the work is not satisfactory, a red dot is placed over the orange, with an explanation of the failed QA status written on a green card that's pinned to the board behind the original card. The original pair will return to that card at the earliest convenient time, put another yellow dot over the red dot, and the cycle begins again.

A lone piece of yarn stretched across the board is moved down, day by day, every morning. If we are right where we thought we'd be on any given day, we'd see only orange and green dots above the string, and no yellow. If there are some yellows, it's clear who may need help from others as the week progresses. Those that have orange and green below the string are most likely helping those who are behind.

Visible Artifacts Encourage Cooperation

We put visible reminders about our process and culture out in the open where everyone can see them. Using the walls in this way avoids the plague of "out of sight, out of mind."

If we are discussing something important, and there is a big visible chart on the wall (or a whiteboard or flip chart) that pertains to our conversation, we can stand up and start pointing and arguing using an obvious visual standard pinned to a nearby wall that all parties must acknowledge—no one is arguing from memory about an ambiguous conversation from last month's meeting. For the programmers, this might be a big chart depiction of a database schema. For our designers, you'll see all kinds of design artifacts out in the open, from mind maps to persona maps to prototype designs. For the whole company, we discovered that *none* of us—including me, the CEO—clearly understood our overall financial performance until we displayed revenue, expenses, and profits on a simple wallboard display for everyone to see and understand.

If we kept this important information as electronic documents stored on a password-protected server, no one would ever look at them. If it was printed on office paper and cataloged in a standard binder on the shelf, no one but the most obsessive team member would ever pull the book off the shelf and bring it into a team conversation about a design idea. Check for yourself: look at your department's three-ring binders and see how much dust has gathered on the top edges of the pages. Go into your document management system and note the last time the document was opened. We cynically refer to these traditional systems as data mausoleums: documents go in; they never come out.

We also use the highest part of the walls at Menlo for important cultural reminders. Not industry-standard motivational posters, but rather handcrafted posters that reflect our most important cultural reminders. The bedrock of our culture is represented by the biggest and oldest poster in our room: "Make Mistakes Faster!"

Storytelling Is a Cultural Conversation

All cultures, ancient and modern, have their own forms of totems, artifacts, and rituals. But there is definitely something magical and affirming in storytelling. It's a cultural tradition that I'm particularly proud we've developed at Menlo.

A reminder to "Make Mistakes Faster."

One evening a few years ago, the team was heading out to the Old Town, a favorite Ann Arbor bar, and they invited me to join them. We sat there on a Friday night for several hours, long after the meal was finished, talking about Menlo and telling stories. At the end of the evening, I apologized to the team for consuming the entire evening talking about Menlo. "Rich, we love talking about Menlo," they replied. And with that they let me off the hook (though I still bought dinner).

Storytelling is also the way I've learned to engage our visiting audience. I like to think of our tours as conversations with visitors, in which they learn of our rituals and artifacts through stories. Over time, we have gained some regular repeat visitors who come back so often with new colleagues that some of them are perfectly comfortable leading parts of the tours themselves. Many of these regulars also have their favorite Menlo stories and prompt their tour guide to repeat them. It's clear they have identified the most important parts of our culture through their favorite stories.

You may believe your company is not compelling and that a tour of your company would be boring. No matter what you do, you have stories from your work life—fun, interesting, compelling stories. Experiment with storytelling as a part of your culture. If you can get the world to start telling your company's stories, you will reinforce your mission every single minute of every single day, even when you are not in the room.

FIVE

Interviewing, Hiring, and Onboarding

Death will be a great relief. No more interviews.

—KATHARINE HEPBURN

The hiring process is a key junction in which to build and foster your culture of joy. In interviewing, hiring, and training a brand-new team member, many companies would like to think they have an opportunity to pick and mold the exact people they want in their company. Yet it's astounding how often it goes so very wrong.

The traditional interview process was always the same for me: two people sitting across from each other and lying to each other for two hours. It went a little something like this . . .

"Are you a team player, Susan?"

"Absolutely. I love people, Rich."

"If you were a day of the week, what day would you be?"

"Monday morning, seven thirty a.m., Rich."

"I love Monday morning people, Susan!"

Then I would go on and on about what a great place this was to work. I'd wax poetic about all our new projects and how Susan would be a perfect fit.

After this fabulous interview, in which we discover that Susan and I are on the same page about absolutely everything from our approaches to teamwork to our favorite local coffee shop, I'd be

thrilled to offer her a job, and she'd be happy to accept. I would often discount any concerns I'd heard about her from my other team
members, as they hadn't gotten a chance to know her as well as I did.

Usually, the best day of any new job is the day of the interview.
On that fateful day, we are both convinced this will be the start of
a new life. But the downward spiral starts quickly—on the first day
on the job. Susan would show up for her first day—and I would be
unprepared.

*Susan? Susan? Oh, yeah, Susan. Today? Really? Shoot. Why didn't
HR get back to me?* I'd only barely remembered that Susan was joining our company today, but I'd have to put on a happy face and go
meet our newest employee.

"Susan, welcome! We're so excited you're here! Hey, listen—
something went wrong in the HR paperwork process and, well, we
aren't quite fully ready for you. I mean, things are just crazy right
now with everything going on. We don't have a cube ready, a phone,
a computer, an e-mail address, business cards. But boy, are we glad
you're here. We are so excited. Welcome!"

Next, I'd walk Susan to the break room and get her set up in
there. "It will be a great way to meet everyone. They all spend a lot
of time here," I'd say. "I'll give you some reading material, including
the product specs for the current product. Don't take them too seriously, though; they are just a little out of date."

As I walked Susan back to the break room, I would pop into
cubes and offices, introducing her to my team. I'm sure they all were
wondering, "Who the hell is this? Who did Rich hire now? I hope
I don't have to slow down and try to teach her something. I've got
deadlines, and a vacation coming up."

Back at the break room, I'd have to jet off to solve another problem but decide to leave Susan with a nice healthy sense of chaos:
"One other thing. You know those projects we discussed during
your interview? The budget hasn't been approved yet. A couple of
them have already been canceled, and a couple of them are delayed

because we are way behind on getting the release of our new product out the door. I was sure it would be done by now, but we caught some important problems in quality testing, and the team can't figure out what's going on because the problems only happen on the testing machines. It's driving everybody crazy. You know how it goes."

Susan feels a strange sense of foreboding and, within minutes of her arrival, begins wondering whether she made a good decision in accepting our job offer. This place feels eerily similar to the place she just left and not at all like the place she heard about during the interview. Susan is no longer quite as sure as she was when she turned in her resignation to her old boss.

Susan then gets to know the testing team in the lunchroom. They're lamenting how far behind they are on the test plan. A revelation occurs to all of them: if Susan joins the testing effort, it would be a great way for her to get to know the product. Susan, the very capable programmer, discovers a problem during testing, so she gets curious and looks at the code around it. After all, she is bored out of her mind, and this makes her feel productive. Suddenly, the team realizes that Susan is a great debugger. Since her projects are never going to see the light of day, she is now stuck in the bug fix team. Hey, at least there is plenty of work.

Usually about six weeks into this process, I overhear Susan complaining in the break room. The job is different from the one she heard about in the interview, and, quite frankly, things were better at her old employer.

Boom. Failure. I was not able to get Susan productive before I demoralized her. And I had the gall to ask, "Why can't I find good people?"

When I relate this story to Menlo guests, some pull me aside and ask me which person at their company have I been talking to, as I had just perfectly described their interview, hiring, and onboarding process. My daughter Lauren once asked me if "Susan's" story was a real story. I told her it absolutely was, because it's everyone's hiring story.

The first few weeks for a new employee are often a hazing ritual comprising boredom and confusion, a rite of passage for the uninitiated.

If you want to create your own version of Joy, Inc., your current screening and interviewing process is likely defeating your intention. I can't say this emphatically enough. Most organizations operate in a default culture defined by: "Whom did we hire?" "What attitudes do they bring to work?" and "What behaviors do we tolerate?" Your culture should be so abundantly obvious in your interview process, it would be impossible for any potential employee to miss. The power of implementing this during your hiring process is that candidates who are poor fits for your intentional culture won't want to work for you. They will easily reject your culture if they sense a clear mismatch with their own personality and desires. The goal of your interviewing process should be to identify bright, capable people who are a good fit for your culture and want it to thrive.

Superstars Need Not Apply

Our interview process aligns strongly with our cultural expectations, so the teaching of our joyful culture happens at first contact. If someone reaches out to us with a desire to join our team, the first thing we do is invite them for a public tour. If they come in for a few hours, see our zany approach, hear about our open and collaborative work environment, find out they won't even have a desk or computer to call their own, and still want to work here, we have a much better chance for a fit.

We are often asked, "Doesn't this mean you might lose out on landing a superstar programmer who needs their private space and library quiet?" Absolutely. We will lose a chance to land these lone genius programmers. They would not fit in at Menlo, and we are both better off for this. A company defines itself by what it chooses to say no to as much as by what it says yes to. Saying no to lone-wolf superstars is an important part of our defining a joyful culture. My career is littered with company geniuses who hoarded knowledge, didn't get along with anybody, and ultimately wrecked the overall team results and morale.

We are trying to build a team, not a collection of individual heroes who can't get along with anybody. The days of individual heroes creating something great in the software industry are long gone. It used to be that two guys could write an operating system in a couple of months—think Bill Gates and Paul Allen in the early eighties. Microsoft had ten thousand people working for nearly five years to build Windows Vista, with a price tag of nearly $10 billion—and we all know how well that turned out. Individual heroes are useless to team building. Don't want 'em. Don't need 'em. Ever. They don't add joy.

Hire Humans, Not Polished Résumés

In 1998, a year before I had started the Java Factory at Interface Systems, I had a very revealing hiring moment. "Sam" had come in to interview for a programmer position. He was the perfect candidate. First of all, he had been referred by someone on my team. (We rewarded staff for referrals—something I've since learned is one of the most terrible HR tactics ever invented if you want an intentionally joyful culture.) His experience was perfect for the role: six years of deep immersion in all the latest Microsoft technologies. He lived right in town, and he wasn't perfectly happy with his current employer. Hiring him would be as easy as shooting a duck on a pond. I figured I could have the position filled that afternoon.

The first few minutes of the interview confirmed my initial instincts about Sam. I liked the guy: he was polished, professional, passionate, and would clearly be a great addition to my team. About halfway through the interview, however, something started going very wrong. Sam's body language shifted entirely. He stopped smiling, pulled his arms across his chest, and sat back in the chair. He seemed disengaged and the answers became mechanical and perfunctory. *He isn't coming to work here after all*, I thought. *What the hell is happening?*

I couldn't let it go on. I stopped the interview and very honestly asked Sam, "What happened here?"

"If I want to just keep doing what I'm doing in my current job, I'll stay there," he said. "I heard you had these cool new Java projects going on. I want to learn new things." Sam confirmed my suspicions that any chance of our hiring him was effectively killed about halfway through our meeting.

This conversation set off an alarm in my brain. No one ever got into a field of work to keep doing the same thing over and over again for their entire career. Yet executives wanted our new team members to hit the ground running. They didn't have time for someone to learn a new skill on our dime. Training was hard enough with my existing team members, and I couldn't afford the time or the investment to teach a new hire a language he or she didn't know.

I didn't get to hire Sam, but I did get something far more valuable from that interview. The exchange made me question everything I knew about hiring. Hiring for skills wasn't going to work. I stopped looking for what people knew and became far more concerned with who potential employees were as human beings.

My experiences with Sam and Susan taught me great and important lessons. I couldn't interview, hire, and onboard the same way I had been. But if I was not going to hire for skills anymore, or stand for the "two people lying to each other for two hours" interview, what *was* I going to do instead?

Your interview needs to match your culture. You shouldn't inter-act with your potential hires differently than you do with your team. Cultures and teams are like families and tribes. Each one has different customs and habits. Each has variations on what is accept-able behavior and what is unacceptable. There is no way to know if there are unresolvable differences during a two-hour interview.

At Menlo we work in close collaboration. Therefore, our first inter-viewing imperative is, "Do you have good kindergarten skills?" Are you respectful? Do you play well with others? Do you share? During what we call our "Extreme Interview," we will mention good kinder-garten skills several times, since it's tantamount to our joyful culture that you play well with others. This is not a theoretical or rhetorical concept. Given we work in pairs all day long, this is crucial.

There are no questions you could ask during a traditional, corporate-style interview that could even remotely determine whether a can-didate was a fit for what we are seeking. Most résumé writers don't go back far enough in their history to share their kindergarten report card. We need a way to test what Mrs. Kleinschmidt taught you in 1983 and figure out whether you remember the most important lessons.

A résumé—full of vague titles, employment periods, compliance ratings, university degrees, and the illuminating "skills section"—is pretty useless for the all-important culture fit imperative, so we don't read very much of it. Traditional résumés speak to the hiring practices of a person's former employers and the admission criteria of the universities they chose to attend. Those evaluation systems are so intrinsically broken, I certainly wouldn't want them to influ-ence my company's culture.

Menlo has better ideas of how to discover who you are as a human being, and we've crafted an interview process in which we don't have to ask any questions of the candidates. Okay, there are two questions: we do need to know that you are at least eighteen years old and you are legally entitled to work in the United States. But other than that, our hiring process is the opposite of what many are familiar with.

Cast a Wide Net

When we're looking to add new people to our team, we cast a wide net and invite all the potential candidates in at once. Our first interview is a mass interview of thirty to fifty people at the same time. This way, we don't have to spend any effort sorting through stacks of résumés and making preliminary decisions based on feeble attempts to catalog human beings by the buzzwords we read on a couple of sheets of paper. An excellent benefit of this approach is that it scales; our interview process doesn't slow down with more people.

These Extreme Interviewing events, as we term them, usually take place two to three times a year, as needed. The day of our interview is very exciting and high energy for our candidates and for us. How many interview processes can claim that? The excitement starts before interviewees arrive as we set up our tables in an arrangement that looks remarkably like a speed-dating session. Menlonians who have volunteered to take part in the process help prepare materials for the various exercises.

As applicants arrive, they are curious and energized by our space. The candidates are about to experience what is essentially a trust-building class before they even start working for us—our version of a ropes course.

We start the mass interview by describing our joyful mission and explaining the importance of an intentional interview process that supports this. Prior to the interview, we send out materials about Menlo, including an *Inc.* magazine cover story that Leigh

Buchanan wrote about Menlo in July 2011 and a detailed white paper so the candidates can read a little bit about our process and culture.

There's no point in surprising anyone or in keeping aspects of our work hidden. We want them to succeed, and transparency helps that. One of our established team members once questioned this cultural openness to our interviewees. If they know about our values, he reasoned, they can mold their behavior to mimic them during our hiring process. "What if they can fake collaboration?" he asked.

James Goebel responded with the obvious. "Can they fake collaboration eight hours a day, every day? Woo-hoo! I'm okay with that."

First Round: Simulate the Work

We start the interview process by telling the candidates that they are going to pair with one another. A Menlonian will be assigned to observe each pair as it works through three exercises. Most of the people will already be aware of our pairing practice, but they don't necessarily expect to jump into it during their first minutes of an interview.

James often emcees the interviewing event. He starts by explaining the first twenty-minute paper-based exercise. For programmers, the first exercise typically involves estimating how many hours it would take to implement the software for a variety of story cards for a fictional project. Many are surprised we don't use computers or coding examples during our interview process. Our exercises are meant to demonstrate teamwork, not technical skill. The purpose, James tells them, is to make your partner look good. If your partner struggles, help him or her out. If you know something the other person doesn't know, share it. The goal is to get your partner a second interview. In these first few minutes the candidates are confronted full force by our cultural values. You can likely imagine the twisting of brains at this point, as candidates want to make sure *they* get the second interview.

The participants are then randomly paired off. For the next twenty minutes the partners quickly disappear into the exercise, overseen by a Menlo observer. The room becomes noisy as everyone is sitting in close proximity to one another, chatting, heads bent over their assignment. Why, it looks like Menlo on any given workday! Some pairs struggle as they try to comprehend it all, while others take to all of this quite naturally.

What becomes quite clear is that people quickly revert to their natural style, even if it doesn't benefit them in this process. We've seen people grab the pencil out of the other person's hand. Others have completely ignored their pair partner, literally turning away from the other person and focusing all their attention on the observer.

The exercises are paper based and don't require a computer or even a calculator. They are not tricky, nor is there a "right" answer—although there are good answers. One exercise requires the pair to decide what features should be selected to fit in the budget for a fictional project, based on the value and relative cost of each of those features (a simulation of our planning game). Another exercise is to create paper and pencil screen designs for imagined users (introducing our High-Tech Anthropology practice).

All the while, the observers watch how each person contributes to the problem solving, how they share, how they argue, how they collaborate, and whether they actually get something done. Throughout it, the observers are asking themselves, "Would I like to pair with this person for a week? Would I feel supported if I were struggling? Would I be able to support them and would they listen if I did? Would I learn something from this person? Would they help me grow?"

We pair off interviewees three times, each time assigning them a new partner and a new observer. We allow twenty minutes for each pairing exercise. It's noisy, it's intense, it's high energy. It's Menlo.

After the pairing test, we wrap up with closing remarks, open the floor to a few minutes of Q&A from the interviewees, and then invite anyone who hasn't done so already to attend a future tour. We also offer the interviewees an opportunity to send me e-mail feedback about their experience. The reward for that extra follow-up effort is that I'll send a book of their choice to their home from a list of our recommendations.

Let the Team Build the Team

After the interviewees leave, our team of observers gathers to discuss what they saw. Remember—if we had thirty people interview, we would have fifteen observers. We talk about each and every interviewee, spending about five minutes per candidate. The central questions: Did we see enough evidence of good kindergarten skills to invite the person in for a second interview? Would the team feel good about pairing with him or her for a day?

The first thing we do is vote with our thumbs. If the three observers for a given candidate all give a thumbs-up, particularly if that thumbs-up is emphatic and enthusiastic, we don't even further discuss the candidate. He or she gets an immediate invite to the second interview. Similarly, if we have three thumbs-down, no discussion, no invite back. We e-mail a dignified and respectful follow-up along with an invitation to try again at a future event.

Of course, the typical vote is mixed and we need to discuss. This turns out to be an awesome conversation about our culture and why a given candidate fits our culture or not. It's a wonderful opportunity to internally reinforce our cultural intentions and to teach our culture to those who are still pretty new to the team. After this discussion, the entire group votes and the vote tallies are recorded.

As CEO and cofounder, I do get a vote and an opinion, but it's not given any greater weight than anyone else's. The fact that I don't have to pair with the people we are inviting to join our team is reason enough for me to not want to override the team's decision. I want the team members to own this process and to advocate for their potential peers.

Second Round: Do Real Work

If a candidate makes it through to the second interview, he or she comes in alone for an entire day. We give the person a one-day paid contract to work on a real client project all day. (We bill the work to the client, who is informed of this ahead of time, at a lower rate.)

The candidate is assigned to pair on a single assignment on one of our projects. All Menlo team members, even those who are relatively new, are potential pair partners for this second-round "interview." In the morning, the candidate may work with Ted, one of our programmers, and then perhaps pair with Vera, another programmer, in the afternoon. It will be the candidate's job to bring Vera up to speed with what happened in the morning, although Ted is also available for questions.

By pairing with the candidate for several hours, Ted and Vera will get a much more pointed sense of the person's programming skills. If the candidate doesn't know the technology we are working with, that's okay. We watch to see whether the candidate is curious, asking questions and learning on the fly, while translating his or her expertise into this unknown territory.

At the end of this one-day contract, the candidate fills out a time sheet and we pay ten dollars an hour for the work. More than pay, though, the person gets a feel for what this pairing thing is really like. Many have heard of it, but few have actually tried it. It's not for everyone and we're okay with that. We believe an interview should give both sides of the table a chance to evaluate fit for culture.

Once the candidate leaves for the day, the two people he or she paired with—Ted and Vera, in this instance—then meet with Carol, the Factory Floor Manager, who coordinates resource planning for all projects across the factory. She asks them a critical question: would you like to pair with this person again? If the feedback from the team is positive, then we invite the person in for a three-week trial. During this paid three-week contract—now at our higher, entry-level rate—the candidate works on real client projects and pairs with at least three other Menlonians.

If the trial goes well, then the person joins the team. We have landed a new Menlonian. The hard work of acclimation is actually accomplished during the Extreme Interviewing process. We've eliminated the dreaded "first day of work" experience you saw with Susan earlier in the chapter.

Of course, there is still much learning and teaching to do as the new person is integrated into our culture. We will still have washouts after these first few weeks, but that is rare.

Jeff J., one of our programmers, reflected on his unique experience interviewing for Menlo:

Rich likes to say that it takes six weeks before the average employee is demoralized after the interview. For me the fall was much quicker. After three weeks of having no work assignments at a job I had taken out of college, while living out a too real and sad version of the movie *Office Space* and generally annoying everyone with my constant begging for something to do, I was fired. The reason given was "not meshing with the team," which in retrospect was perfectly accurate. Luckily, Menlo was kind enough to allow me to come in for my one-day interview after I had been let go from this joyless job. In a no-longer-in-Kansas-style contrast, the first twenty minutes of my coming into Menlo (it probably would have been closer to five minutes, but I went and got some coffee first), I had my hands on the keyboard, I was working on real code, on a real project, for a real client. By the end of my first day of work, I had met the clients that were paying us to develop their software. By the end of my three-week trial, I was working with people who had started their trial at the exact same time as me. I had found that thing everyone hopes for beyond simply collecting a paycheck: I had found a career. I had also found joy.

Don't Delay in Making Hiring Decisions

The washout rate from our first-round interview can be as high as 60 percent, and the washouts from the second and third phase can be as high as 50 percent. If we bring in fifty people in the first mass interview, the fifty becomes twenty, then ten, then five. We make all of these decisions quickly and rather effortlessly. We don't spend a lot of time worrying about mistakes along the way.

I believe one of the key reasons that most firms face hiring challenges is that their interview process takes too darn long. Once a great candidate is identified, the bureaucracy of HR kicks in. It takes weeks for the candidate to hear back from a company, and by the time the offer is extended the candidate has found another position elsewhere. Our process is fast and catches people while they are still excited.

I recall one California CIO asking, "Rich, am I hearing you correctly? You get fifty people to interview for five positions?" He went on to tell me that he couldn't find five people to show up for fifty positions. I hear the same stories from local executives here in Ann Arbor. "Where do you find people? I can't find people to fill our two open positions."

With an obvious culture and an interview process tuned to that culture, my experience is that recruiting is easy. We might put some clever "sticker" on the home page of our Web site, but that's about it. Word of mouth brings in a lot of people; our reputation precedes us. We usually get fifty people scheduled for an interview with no effort at all. Unlike my management peers at other companies, we are not looking for the perfect someone with the exact skills. At Menlo, we are looking for able learners with curiosity. We can teach skills all day long. If they have a decent foundation, teaching is trivial.

From Lisa H., a longtime project manager at Menlo:

Reflecting on why I find joy in our hiring process—a few things that stand out:

1. We're never "stuck" with someone who is dragging us down, hurting the team. (Everyone at Menlo knows the interview process never stops no matter how long you've been here.) There is joy in that we have the right people for our team.

2. There is joy from the very beginning as the team is getting to help mentor new people.

3. I find a lot of joy in the Extreme Interview events for the social aspect of it, just getting to hang out with the team, and

there are always lots of laughs as we self-reflect on our own faults when we are sharing our feedback on all the candidates. We know we still have lots of work to do to become the team we really want to be.

A Birdcage Without Bars

Despite our best efforts and our thoughtful interviews, hiring still doesn't always work out the way we hope. There must be time and space for adjustment to our unique way of working. People can and do change, given the opportunity. Just as important, though, is that we can't be afraid to let someone go if they ultimately don't fit into our culture. Not all will succeed. If we do have to let someone go, we do so with dignity and respect. It should never be easy to fire people.

We will make mistakes in both directions. We will let people go we shouldn't and hold on to mismatches longer than we should. We are human, after all. But we make one point as clearly as we can: if it didn't work out this time, for whatever reason, you can try again. We are a birdcage without bars. People have gone through our interview process several times before they make it in. Others come back a few times before it becomes evident to both the team and the individual that, even though we may want it, Menlo is not the right fit. Still others come, stay for a while, leave, and come back. While we are often sad to see longtimers move on, we know that it is a natural part of a healthy culture and befits a team whose central theme is to honor the whole life of each team member. (You'll see more of our views on attrition in chapter eleven.)

The open birdcage can have surprising benefits, including marketing your firm. I'm reminded often of Burt, who worked through his three-week trial. He was a good guy and we really liked him, but he just wasn't coming up the learning curve as fast as we needed. It might have been us or it might have been him. More than likely, it was a little bit of both.

Our team decided to cut the cord. Burt had tears. Not too many, but just some welling up at eye corners. Burt really wanted to work for us and we really liked him. A couple of weeks after we let him go, I got a call from him.

"Hey, Rich . . . I just wanted to call and let you know I found a new job in Detroit."

I was so glad he had landed safely in a new job. I told Burt it was very thoughtful of him to call and tell me.

"Oh, no—that's not why I called. We have a software project here that I think would be perfect for Menlo, and I wanted to bring my CEO out for a tour and a discussion."

I guess we handled that exit pretty well. Within days, Burt was in the office with his new CEO, visiting and discussing business with the place that had let him go only a few weeks before.

Whom Do We Need on Our Bus?

Jim Collins, author of *Good to Great*, has a well-known adage about having the right people on the bus and the wrong people off the bus. Our bus at Menlo has many stops—but it has the right people on the bus at the right time.

So what kind of people are on our bus? What roles do we need to fill? Obviously, for our kind of work, we need programmers, but even though our product is working software, programmers are no more than half our team. It takes a lot more than programming to create beautifully designed and solid software. Menlo also needs quality advocates, people who keep the big picture in their head and make sure everything fits together as work progresses. We also need project managers, who keep everything organized and are the point people for our clients.

Then there are the folks on our team with the pretty cool title you've already seen a few times—our High-Tech Anthropologists, or HTAs. Theirs is the role missing from almost every other software team on the planet—and many other companies as well. The work of our High-Tech Anthropologists makes all the difference in delighting the users of the software we are building.

The Power of Observation

Discovery is seeing what everyone else has seen, and thinking what no else has thought.

—ALBERT SZENT-GYÖRGYI,
Nobel Prize–winning Hungarian physiologist

One Saturday morning, I was out running errands and stopped by the hardware store to pick up a bag of topsoil. Loading my car in the parking lot, I was approached by the owner of the car I was blocking in. I was about to apologize for the inconvenience when he pointed at the logo on my T-shirt. It was the logo for Accuri Cytometers, one of our key clients. He exclaimed, "I use that product every day. I *love* that product."

"Oh, yeah?" I said. "We built the software."

"You guys did a great job. You made my life so much easier compared to the other product I used to use. Thank you."

I loaded the rest of the bags of topsoil and was on my way, with a joyful spring in my step. His response was a clear sign that High-Tech Anthropology worked, that our team had designed a usable program for the users.

The very essence of our joy at Menlo comes from the delight people experience in using the software we create. The goal is always the same: design and build software that is usable without manuals, training classes, or help text. We achieve this even in difficult domains where we have had no experience whatsoever.

A company doesn't exist to serve its own people; a company exists to serve the needs of the people who use its products or services. Thinking of joy in this context focuses everyone on a valuable external goal. Software delivery is hard. Coding is exacting, and getting to the right design takes patience and persistence. This is all really hard work and not necessarily happily done at every moment. We get frustrated, we're impatient, there are unexpected problems to resolve. Our joy comes from the outcome of all this hard work. We want to delight the people whose lives are impacted by the software we design and build.

You have a version of this joy in your work. Your job is to pursue that. If your company is an auto manufacturer, your joy might come in hearing drivers use the word *love* when they talk about their car. If you are a deli owner, your joy could come from the groans of satisfied lunch guests who rave about your corned beef on rye. If you are a doctor, you long to build caring, lasting relationships with your patients and keep them healthy and active so they can enjoy every ounce that life has to offer.

Is it possible to systematically get these kinds of wonderful results? Is there a way to organize observation, discovery, and "design" iteratively, so that when things aren't working the way they need to, the obvious and subtle problems are discovered early and promptly designed out of the system, product, or service?

Yes. In order to systematically pursue joy in the name of offering delight to your customers, you must learn to look at the world through a lens that sees problems as opportunities.

The Missing Link

At Menlo, our revelation came when we realized something fundamental was missing from most software teams. If our joyful goal was to delight end users, then we had to invent a new process that kept this end user ever present. We saw that most people, even if they don't work for a high-technology company, are still tortured by software. Your company, like so many others, can't function without software. A service station can't sell gas without using software. A cable company can't offer hundreds of channels without software.

The problem is that there's a missing link when it comes to creating a great experience with software. To fully appreciate what is missing, we first have to understand that the source of this trouble is a fundamental misunderstanding between two vastly different cultures and their competing goals. Software users and software creators speak different languages. They live in different worlds.

The old view saw that one side of software was populated by people like me: *Homo logicus.* We know how computers work and we think they're fun. There is a CPU and RAM; there are hard drives and flash drives. There are SIM cards and USB ports. There is 802.11n and Ethernet. Have you heard of Ruby on Rails? It's the language that made Web 2.0 possible. A few of us are still on the fence about HTML5, but it does show some promise. If you learn to think as I do, all of this will make sense. Once you understand how to think as I do, the software you are struggling to understand will all make sense, too.

On the other side are those pesky users, the stupid users, the *Dummies.* Software creators have been in control for so long now that they have convinced nontechnical people to self-identify as stupid users. This self-deprecation becomes a common excuse when a Web site, or a smartphone, or a digital camera isn't working as expected: "Oh, I'm just a stupid user. I'm sure it's easy—I just haven't taken the time to learn it." Some users, though, begin to wonder why they must think like programmers to understand computers.

So what's missing?

Anthropology is the link. We need to study people in their native environment to figure out how to bring them utility and joy.

Anthropology is the science of humanity. It is concerned with social systems, artifacts, vocabulary, interactions across a community, and the intersections of different groups within a community. Anthropologists need to understand history in order to better understand the present, and in order to do that they explore old historical artifacts; it is somewhat akin to the work of archaeologists. They want to understand people and their stories through a true and unbiased lens, to the extent that is possible.

We believe anthropology must be applied to software design. Using anthropology and making it a vital part of our process helps end the frustration of both our frontline technical folks and those poor users. (Not to mention, it's good for our bottom line.)

The techniques and approaches we use can be applied to any kind of product or service; they have nothing to do with software specifically. My stories and examples will be software stories because that is what we do, but you will be able to extrapolate these stories into your domain.

The Persona

High-Tech Anthropology starts with understanding the people who are going to use the software we are creating. We have to find these people in their native environment, because design is contextual. Focus groups don't work for this because they quickly devolve into dominant personality disorder groups, with one strong voice drowning out all others. And you can't invite users into your office and ask them what they want, because they don't actually know what they want. It's not because they are stupid; it's quite the opposite. They are unconsciously competent at what they do all day, so they can no longer deliver the most important minute details simply because they are unaware of them. The only way to get around this limitation is through keen and patient observation.

Let's say you're a Menlo High-Tech Anthropologist asked to be part of a team that's building a wedding planning Web site, MyAwesomeWedding.com. One of the first questions our team will ask to find out who our user will be is, "What kind of people plan weddings?"

Quickly, you and your teammates would come up with a list: brides, mothers of brides, bridesmaids, sisters of brides, professional wedding planners . . . and *maybe* grooms, too.

The first job of the HTA team, which also works in pairs, is to find these people in their native environment. But where could you go? Churches and synagogues, banquet halls, bridal shows, the bridal magazine rack at Barnes & Noble, jewelry stores, cake shops, and bridal gown and tuxedo shops are all good choices. The team members would conduct casual observation and conversational interviews with people they meet, noting what they see and hear. They'd ask a variety with questions, starting with, "When's the big day?" and uncover whatever other information they could get.

Upon returning to the office, the HTAs begin distilling what they learned into groupings based on the different types of people they found. They encountered young, first-time brides, and women getting married for the second time. They found that mothers-in-law were sometimes involved, as well as sisters, even if they weren't bridesmaids. They also learned that this event might be slightly more important to Mom than to daughter. Once they distill their findings, they can begin to write stories in order to create an artifact called a "persona," which identifies the main user of the system. It might look something like this:

Kathleen Tober is a fifty-two-year-old homemaker from Dexter, Michigan, who will soon help plan her daughter's wedding. She is active and enjoys various community interests and likes to kayak on the Huron River. She bought a new computer last year but doesn't use it as much as she thought she would . . .

Kathleen's goals are:

- Help plan the wedding of the century!

- Determine whether using her computer can save her time. She wants to discuss her computer accomplishments with her daughter.

- Avoid situations where people use terms she doesn't understand, as it makes her feel stupid.

Of course, there is no one person the HTAs met along the way named Kathleen Tober. However, there are elements of truth sprinkled throughout the Kathleen persona, based on what was learned about the audience through observation and interview.

The HTAs will create a couple of dozen personas based on all the different *types* of people they met. These personas represent the keys to the kingdom of joy for a software product. Or, better put, exactly *one* of these personas holds *the* key to the land of joy. The question is, which one?

This is the most difficult question of all, not because there is a right answer, but because the answer is "Pick *one*." At all costs, we must avoid letting our clients fall into the trap of not picking a persona. In forcing them to pick, we hear the same objections every time: "We want this software to work for everyone. We don't want to choose a single persona as the primary persona. We want to dominate this market." If you try to build any product or service to make it work for everyone, it won't work well for anyone in particular, and you will get killed in the market.

We write down all of the possible personas on pieces of card stock roughly the size of an oversized baseball card. Once complete, we hand the stack of personas to our client and walk them over to a large Foamcore board. The board has three concentric rings drawn in the form of an archery target. We then ask the client to make a tough decision by identifying who the primary persona will be for our efforts. They need to pick the main person for whom we will design the planned system or product.

As they look through the cards, every customer has the same lament: all the personas should go in the bull's-eye portion of the persona map. They argue with us. They argue with one another. They try one and then change their mind. They argue some more and then, finally, choose a persona, and we tape it down in the center of the bull's-eye drawn on the Foamcore board. It usually takes hours to get to this point; it's that hard and that important. We then ask the client to pick two secondary personas for the middle ring of the target and three personas for the outside ring.

This persona map becomes the central artifact of our design efforts for that project. Any screens, any buttons, any reports, any features are all evaluated through the lens of the primary persona. We bring this person to life. In the case of MyAwesomeWedding. com, Kathleen Tober would be our primary persona. The marketing team for that Web site decided that it was Mom who controlled the budget and therefore the spending. Amy, the bride, is in the second ring and a secondary persona.

Now, when the HTAs are contemplating designing a button for the MyAwesomeWedding.com screen, they will ask, "How will this work for Kathleen?" If someone responds, "Oh, this feature is for Amy," that's okay, but then the question becomes, "How can we add this feature for Amy so it doesn't interfere with Kathleen's use?" Again, Kathleen is the primary persona. If it doesn't work for Kathleen, we don't have a design.

This kind of attention to our end user's persona makes our work personal, not abstract. We care deeply about how Kathleen will interact with our product and how it will help her life.

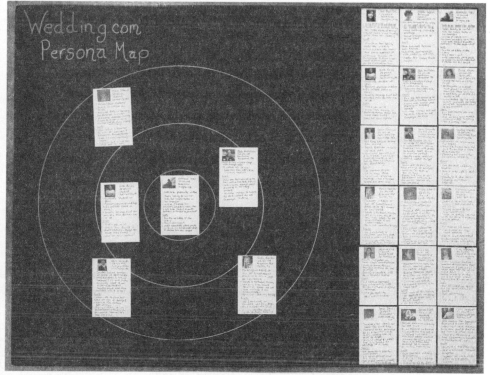

An example of a persona map, with the primary persona in the center of the target.

High-Tech Anthropologists Are Good for Business

One of our favorite HTA experiences occurred during the Accuri flow cytometer persona mapping exercise. Accuri really wanted to dominate their market. They were backed by almost $30 million of venture capital and needed to deliver great returns for their investors.

At first, the Accuri team wanted to put *all* the personas in the center. Of course they did. We pushed back. We told them they had to pick one. They grimaced and ultimately picked Emily, the lab director who currently used the competitors' products. They told us that Emily wouldn't let her graduate assistant (a persona we named Brad) use the flow cytometers already on the market, as mistakes were routine and the cost of an error was too high.

We played a what-if game with them. We asked, "What if we made the software easy enough for Brad to use?" That touched off a firestorm of argument. First, they got angry with us. Emily wouldn't stand for it, they argued. She won't let Brad use it. She won't trust Brad to use it. After several hours, including an overnight time-out away from our team, the Accuri team came back and told us they'd come to an important realization: There were ten times as many Brads as there were Emilys in the market as potential users. Brad should be the primary persona. They made the switch, and we made the software easier to use for the Brads of the world.

In less than three years after the launch of the product, Accuri became a formidable competitor in the flow cytometry market. In February 2011, Accuri was sold to one of their largest competitors for $205 million. We like to think it's because they understood their users better, thanks to High-Tech Anthropology.

High-Tech Anthropologists Observe and Empathize

We were asked to design the user experience for a handheld touch screen for a diesel motor diagnostic tool. Our HTAs went first to the Ann Arbor Transportation Authority to watch Ken, a bus mechanic, do repair work on a bus. The first thing Ken did was put on rubber gloves. Our HTAs noted this and later asked Ken if he wore them all the time. He said that gloves were pretty much standard now for everyone who did this type of work.

This surprised our team. The device being built for Ken and his colleagues, as requested by the client, was going to be a capacitive touch screen display (as on iPhones), which meant it wouldn't work for someone wearing latex gloves. Our customer was also quite surprised by this. Menlo had been in this domain for two hours and discovered something that would have killed the adoption of their product in the marketplace. This was something that the customer, with thirty years of experience in the field, didn't even know about. The problem was solved by switching to a resistive touch screen that responds to the pressure of a finger touch.

Dedicated and careful observation picked up this problem before we went too far into the design process. But HTAs aren't only there to observe physical interactions with our designs. People's work isn't all about going through the motions, after all. Our mental states and deep emotions are also key to understanding how we can build joy into our offerings.

At a county clerk's office for a systems redesign, our HTAs observed that there were picture postcards tacked up all around the office. They observed that the clerks didn't always have the best interactions with citizens, many of whom came in with a chip on their shoulder because they thought taxes in the county were too high. Of course, these clerks had nothing to do with taxes, but that didn't matter to the citizen-customers. The clerks used the postcards as blood pressure medication, imagining themselves in the idyllic beach scenes after difficult exchanges with belligerent customers.

Our HTAs noticed this and placed some of these beach scenes on the home screen of the design. They purposely added stress relief to the system the clerks used every day. Attention to such a small detail deeply touched the clerks. On seeing those beach scenes on their screen, some of the clerks became teary, saying no one had ever listened to them like that before.

The clerks never asked for the beach scenes. But our team observed the way the clerks worked in their natural environment and thought it would be a nice addition to the software that acknowledged the human users of the system. And it really was.

Hand-Drawn Mock-Ups: The Artifacts of the HTAs

Perhaps unsurprisingly, our High-Tech Anthropology system comes with its own set of artifacts that are as important as our story cards and estimation sheets.

The High-Tech Anthropologists work in pairs to create simple, low-fidelity, hand-drawn screen mock-ups for the product they're working on. If the design is a Web site or app, then the mock-ups are drawn on paper that is the same size as the screen of the typical device, whether it's a computer monitor, an iPad screen, or an Android phone. If the client is building special hardware, say, for a diagnostic tool, we often start our projects when the imagined hardware is nonexistent except as a blueprint specification. In this case,

A paper-based prototype for our "Dragonfly" project.

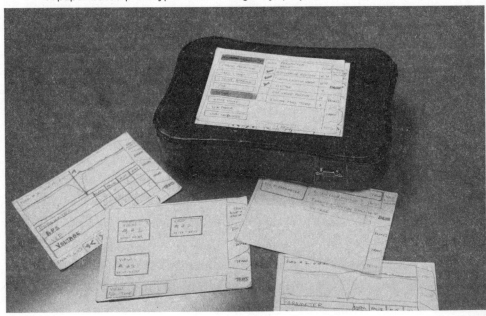

our mock-ups will include physical prototypes, sometimes made out of duct tape and cardboard.

These paper-based, hand-drawn, user experience design prototypes are then tested against real-world users. The High-Tech Anthropologists have the users play with the prototype. Rather than ask them what they think about the draft design, we ask them to use the prototype to complete a task while we observe this use. For example, with the diesel motor diagnostic tool we helped design, we handed a diesel motor technician a duct-taped physical prototype along with a paper-screen mock-up properly positioned on the model and asked him what he would do to perform an initial diagnostic test. We were looking to see whether the end user would know how to use it without help. By using simple, often crude physical prototypes to simulate hardware and hand-drawn screen mock-ups to evoke the display, virtually everyone we test with will play with these nonthreatening examples.

You might be surprised that we are a software company that relies so heavily on paper-based systems. One Menlo visitor sternly told me he lost all faith in us based on this "compromise," because he saw our use of paper to plan and do our work as a failure of our software acumen.

It's not that simple. We choose the tools we believe work better for the humans. Sometimes electronic is best, but often it is not, particularly for a team whose members all sit in the same room together. Humans are visual creatures with a high preference for tactile tools—and paper is still more tactile than touch screens. It would cost millions of dollars in hardware and software development to match the flexibility and scalability of our paper-based systems, and it still wouldn't be as useful or effective. Our democratic ideals play into these paper-based tools as well. Uncomplicated tools that are easy to learn invite wider participation by all stakeholders.

Design for Living

Whatever you do for a living, design plays a role. A restaurant should have a great menu and customer experience. A university should make it easy for students to apply, register for classes, and pay their bills. An airline should make it easy to reserve a seat and print a boarding pass.

To succeed in design, a company must define its target audience and be very specific. If you look back at the persona for Kathleen, reflect on the fact that her goals have nothing to do with technology; rather they have everything to do with her as a person.

Kathleen's goals:

Help plan the wedding of the century!

She wants to create a wonderful memory for her family.

Determine whether using her computer can save her time. She wants to discuss her computer accomplishments with her daughter.

She wants meaningful conversations with her daughter.

Avoid situations where people use terms she doesn't understand, as it makes her feel stupid.

She doesn't want to feel stupid through any of this because that negative feeling would last a lifetime.

———

In order to meet your persona's goals, you need to iterate your designs: make a small, simple design, test it with real users, refine, and repeat. You don't need to have design intuition to win with design. You simply need to be a keen observer of human behavior, stay humble when your brilliant designs don't work, and be willing to adjust your designs as often as needed to get to a joyful user experience.

Scouting a High-Tech Anthropologist

Many wish to know where we find our High-Tech Anthropologists. Well, not in the anthropology department at universities. It's not that we wouldn't look there; we just haven't had a lot of luck doing so when we tried. We actually find HTAs in every walk of life. Those who have worked for us have had quite varied backgrounds: elementary school teachers, journalists, floral department managers, housekeeping managers, industrial operations engineers, film majors, to name a few.

What do we look for? In addition to the standard kindergarten talents already discussed for all Menlonians, HTAs must also possess a wide range of talents including:

- Great observation skills
- The ability to sit quietly at times
- A "make mistakes faster" attitude
- User interface design skills
- Ability to draw with crayons and markers
- Ability to use Post-it notes
- Expertise in Photoshop (ironically, a very complicated piece of software from Adobe)
- Empathy
- Ability to deal with ambiguity and abstraction
- Ability to create with specificity and exactness

Knowing how to code is not a requirement.

There's no way to test for these skills, so we use our best discernment during Extreme Interviewing, pair them with our best teachers while doing real work, and see if they have what it takes. No one is training High-Tech Anthropologists for us. We had to develop our own. By introducing anthropology into your work, you can, too.

SEVEN

Fight Fear, Embrace Change

Fear is the mind-killer.

—BENE GESSERIT, "Litany Against Fear," from Frank Herbert's *Dune*

Fear is one of the biggest killers of joy. That's why, early on in our factory experiments, James Goebel would declare that anything that went wrong at Menlo was his fault. Ted, one of our most senior programmers, picked up on this concept right away. Any time something didn't work out, Ted would say, "It's James's fault!" This little quip freed the team from faultfinding and allowed everyone to work on the problem rather than seeking someone to blame.

Freedom from fear requires feeling safe. If you feel safe, you run experiments. You stop asking permission. You avoid long, mind-numbing meetings. You create a new kind of culture in which you accept that mistakes are inevitable. You learn that small, fast mistakes are preferable to the big, slow, deadly mistakes you are making today.

Most organizations give lip service to "Fail fast." During early experiments when a team is testing their limits, it doesn't take much to crush their spirit, and then, suddenly, experiments become all about *being safe*, not taking small risks. In a *being safe* culture, people choose to run safe experiments that they know will succeed, effectively exhausting the energy behind a change initiative. This kind of practice is deadly to innovation.

It's the opposite of a *feeling safe* culture. To establish a *feeling safe* culture, you must first come to grips with the fact that you are asking the people on your team to be vulnerable in ways that society has systematically drummed out of us since youth. Think about the common wisdom: "Earn good grades." "Get into a good college." "Find a good job." "Get a promotion." "Earn more." Perhaps somewhere along the way, you tried something radical and it didn't work. You ended up with a lousy grade that knocked down your grade point average. That prevented you from getting into Stanford. So you didn't get the job at Google and you are not a multimillionaire today. You failed.

And now we're asking you to go fail faster.

Make Mistakes Faster

Our earliest experiment with Bob J. and Clare at Interface Systems was in testing Extreme Programming. Although I initially wanted to try all these crazy techniques with the whole team, we started with one pair working for a few weeks. We ran a small experiment that wouldn't have brought down the entire team if it didn't work. Once it was evident that the experiment was successful at the two-person level, we then ran the second small experiment, the one-week trial in the Java Factory.

I know many organizations take a "burn the boats" approach to change. They try huge experiments that are given no room for failure. This can work really well if you are absolutely right about your decision, and it can be disastrous if you are not. In order to try anything really new, you should start small. Small gives you space to run cheap experiments that barely register if they don't work out.

If a *make mistakes faster* culture is going to survive and thrive, you must establish a standard of fast, frequent, and inexpensive experimentation. Assume that many of your first experiments will fail. One of the most common phrases you'll hear at Menlo is "Let's run the experiment." We are apt to say that at least once a day. We don't count experiments and we don't track success/failure rates, but if we did, we would look for success and failure rates to be about even. If the percentage of failures started dropping, we'd become concerned that fear had crept into the room and that people weren't taking those important risks.

Avoid the Deadly Paralysis of Sunk-Cost Thinking

In its simplest form at Menlo, our programming pairs will experiment by writing some code to see if something works or not. If it does not, they will throw the code away and start over. I know this sounds simple, particularly to people who don't do this for a living, but you can't imagine the sunk-cost mentality that can go into just a few lines of code already typed in.

Sunk-cost thinking is one of the most insidious obstacles to change in business today. "Sunk cost" simply refers to the money already invested in a project. If we decide later an endeavor was a mistake, we worry that all of that money has been wasted. This sunk-cost thinking paralyzes teams into one or more of three equally deadly forms of inaction.

The first inaction is "We've already invested so much in our current system" and consequently it would seem insane to change it. If we make it over that mental hurdle, then we face the second type of inaction that results from wanting to avoid the possibility of a future failure and its sunk cost. I've watched large teams of people spend hours, sometimes days, in a conference room arguing whether or not a simple one-hour experiment should be tried. The argument goes something like this: "Yeah, but if this doesn't work out, then we'd have wasted our time." Perhaps, even more important, they are thinking, "And I might be seen as someone who tries stuff that doesn't work." If there is this much resistance to small changes, imagine the inertial force at work in contemplating big ones.

If an experiment actually gets off the ground, the third deadly form of inaction will consume every molecule of organizational might: the inaction of not changing course, even when it's clear the experiment has failed, for fear that we will have to consider everything invested so far a loss. Once a course is set, teams double down all their bets and keep going, even though they know they are headed for failure.

Consider the Ford Everest project, a massive effort in the dot-com age to consolidate some thirty disparate purchasing and procurement systems into one Web-based system that would serve multiple tiers of suppliers. In 2004, Ford finally canceled the doomed IT project after it had invested $400 million in it. Can you imagine how hard it would have been to cancel a project after $100 million was spent? They likely declared that another $100 million would get it back on track, then another $200 million, and then . . . canceled, with $400 million down the drain. Apparently, yet another $200 million was then needed, not to finish it, but to undo it and get back to where they'd started. I figure you have to manufacture and sell one million vehicles to generate $600 million of free cash flow just to cover the cost of one failed IT initiative. And you know this isn't the only failed project within this one company.

Ford hasn't somehow captured the market of failed IT initiatives, especially within the automotive industry. This is an epidemic of epic proportions.

Years ago, I led a seminar for a major university's health system on the top six reasons software projects fail and how to avoid them. After I got through the list, someone in the group raised his hand and said, "Oh, we had one of those. We failed on all six points, after $30 million was spent. And that was the second time we failed. The first time we spent $18 million." Nearly $50 million with nothing to show for it. That project failure had been discussed in the local press, so I didn't feel I was sharing any secrets when I referred to it during a later public presentation. Someone with that university's badge approached me after my talk. "Rich, which of the four projects at the university that failed were you referring to? I couldn't tell from your description." It was even worse than I had known. The university hadn't spent $50 million on one failed project but $200 million on four failed initiatives! This is where sunk-cost thinking takes you.

Every industry has its own version of such failures that come from dangerous sunk-cost thinking. Why is it important to think about massive failure in your pursuit of joy? Simply put, sunk-cost thinking paralyzes organizations into making really big mistakes very slowly. They attempt to avoid bad news by pretending it doesn't exist. Ignoring the simple fact of human nature that people hate to confront bad news, especially big bad news, will confound your pursuit of joy, as it will defeat many change initiatives before they even start. There is fear just in the idea of change.

The Cost of Artificial Fear

When management manufactures *artificial* fear as part of the management of its people, sunk-cost thinking acts like an amplifier to this manufactured fear.

What does artificial fear look like? It can be as simple as a row of raised executive eyebrows when you point out that something isn't going as expected at a Monday morning status meeting. It could be as serious as bad news stopping with a certain executive because the next level up makes it clear that failure is not an option. Roger M. Boisjoly, a former insider at Morton Thiokol, Inc., the maker of the infamous booster rockets and suspect O-rings that led to the explosion of the space shuttle *Challenger*, offered the following thoughtful analysis of artificial fear at that company: "Many opportunities were available to structure the workforce for corrective action, but the MTI management style would not let anything compete or interfere with the production and shipping of boosters."

Bad news can hide for a long, long time, but it doesn't go away simply because we manufacture artificial fear. The fear and the associated hidden sunk cost just go underground and pollute the groundwater of the organization's cultural and financial ecosystems. As with the MTI example, the results can sometimes be deadly.

For a *make mistakes faster* culture to thrive, you must remove manufactured fear as a management tool. I like to think of our approach at Menlo as a cultural HVAC system. We pump fear out of the room, filter out ambiguity, adjust the cultural temperature to the setting that makes the team comfortable, and then pump safety back in.

When we pump fear out of the room and give the team permission to make mistakes, the team starts to feel safe. If team members feel safe, they will begin to trust one another. If they trust one another, they will begin to collaborate and we see teamwork. When mistakes are made, the team owns up to the mistake because there is no fear of reprisal or penalty. No time or human energy is wasted by organizing a posse to nab the culprit.

Fear comes with a high cost. Fear causes the body to release two powerful chemicals: adrenaline and cortisol. The physiological effect of these two chemicals is that blood is channeled to the muscles and away from the learning centers of the brain. The fearful brain operates purely out of the amygdala, or as some refer to it, the reptile brain. Fight or flight are our only options. We've closed off our access to creativity and innovation. We've closed off the opportunity for change.

There is an another path, one chosen infrequently in most organizations: run a series of small experiments within a culture of safety. The easiest way to describe this approach is to say, "Let's try this and see what happens." If it works, do more of it. If it doesn't, change it or do less. We'd rather fail fast than not test.

Experiment: Planning Origami

During the Java Factory days at Interface Systems, we made a lot of improvements in overall productivity, quality, and speed, yet we were still not able to constrain the requirements in a tangible way that allowed us to hit our budget and time frames. I started paying more attention to the product manager who worked with us every other week to set priorities, and I noticed something subtle. He was always requesting an excess of forty hours of estimated work per resource on my team. I knew this wasn't sustainable.

"Oh, it's just one more little thing," he would say, in a slightly high-pitched, whiny way. I told him I would be happy to tell my team they were now on fifty-hour workweeks, but he assured me he didn't want my team working more. He just wanted them to get more done.

In many projects, one of the deadliest challenges is scope creep. The easiest way to describe scope creep is that it's the infamous addition of "It's just one more little thing," often brought up in hallway conversations by people who don't have to do the work. Add in enough "just one more thing's" and voilà! The deadline is missed and the project is over budget. Most Dilbert comics emanate from scope creep, typically initiated by the pointy-haired boss.

James suggested we run an experiment to combat this particular product manager's scope creep and plan how we would use our forty hours each week. He recommended folding photocopies of the task cards to the size of the estimate for that task. A 5½-by-8½-inch copy would mean that that task card would require sixteen hours of work. That same card folded in half would mean eight hours would be needed for that task. This card folded in half again would indicate four hours, and one more fold, two hours. A thirty-two-hour card would be taped to a full-size sheet of paper, making it twice as big as a sixteen-hour card. Easy to create, easy to understand.

We then created tabloid-size planning sheets with an inscribed box that could hold forty hours' worth of folded cards. Our product manager picked up the folded cards and placed them inside the inscribed box. He could place up to forty hours of task card time on the sheet—but no more. This puzzle was simple enough that the product manager, after using the system for just a few weeks, seldom asked for "just one more thing." When he did, we asked him what he would like to remove to make enough room for the new card. He didn't necessarily like it, but this experiment stopped scope creep in its tracks.

Most of our experiments at Menlo look something like this project planning origami experiment: simple, inexpensive, and fast. Many experiments don't survive for very long because they don't solve the problem. Some are only needed temporarily; others start as temporary and become permanent. We think many are amazing solutions to long-standing problems when, in reality, they last for a little while and then change or go away. Then we run a new experiment.

Incrementally Change a Current Process and Give It Time

A big part of the joy in running small experiments is that you don't have to make a final decision on anything right away. This is different from ambiguity, when people on the team are never sure whether a decision has been made and, if so, what the decision is. In this case, we are unambiguously modifying a part of our process, but also reserving the right to unambiguously change our mind later if things aren't working.

The Wilmut project is one of our biggest projects to date. The work involves designing and developing software for an FDA-validated medical diagnostic device. We routinely have more than twenty people on this project. During weekly project kickoff sessions, we walk through all the planned cards together before each pair starts working on its assigned cards. With Wilmut, the team struggled with having so many people working together and so many cards to get through, so we ran a few different experiments intended to improve the kickoffs.

Some team members weren't excited about the different ideas, such as splitting the project team into two separate groups of ten people each during kickoff and discussing a subset of the cards in each group. The team removed the fear of these changes by suggesting we try something for a week or two and reflect on the results. We could always do something else if we really didn't like how it worked out. Our team is willing to try an experiment if some members on the team are passionate about it. We don't need to have full buy-in just to start an experiment.

Another team member further reinforced this notion by saying we should do the same thing for at least two to three weeks in a row before making any judgments on how the experiment had gone. To truly run an experiment, you need to try something out more than once, because at first—no matter what you try—it will probably be bumpy.

Experiment: Clients in the Office

Every now and then we'd have a client team or even a potential client in the factory when standup was called. I'm sure at the beginning there were some awkward moments on both sides, as we didn't necessarily want to make our clients attend this goofy style of meeting. But James offered to run the small experiment of including the client team, if present, in the standup. Even though we weren't sure how this would be embraced, we went ahead and invited them into the standup circle. Without a hitch, they all played right along. When the Viking helmet token was passed to them, they would participate in the report, telling the team what they were working on back in the office, what troubles they were facing, and where they needed help. It was fun and affirming for our mission.

We have one client, Linda, who is now so taken with our systems, including standup, that she has jokingly asked if she is going to get a paycheck for the amount of time she spends with us. I assured her this wouldn't be a problem, if she wouldn't mind seeing her name on the invoices we sent her. She does volunteer to help us with portions of her project where she can add value, particularly with testing. On one level, it saves her money on her project—she is a sole proprietor—but on another level, she also appreciates the rapport it builds with her software team. What began as an awkward corporate social experiment in the end reinforced the transparency of our culture.

Experiment: International Interns

Our first office at Menlo was a small, street-level storefront in the historic Kerrytown District of downtown Ann Arbor. In the summertime, we often left our front door open and folks would peek in and ask what we were doing. We'd lead them on an informal tour, and these informal tours caused word about this weird company called Menlo Innovations to spread quickly.

One day a student, Esha Krishnaswamy, walked into our office. She was part of an international organization at the University of

Michigan called IAESTE, the International Association for the Exchange of Students for Technical Experience. Esha asked if Menlo would be interested in hosting an international intern for up to a year. It seemed like a complicated concept for a small start-up firm, but she assured me it was a very simple process. We needed to fill out a two-page job description, pay an application fee, and IAESTE would take care of the rest.

It all sounded too good to be true, but with our pairing approach, it would be easy to bring an intern up to speed and integrate him or her into the team. Although I was worried about onboarding an international intern, Esha assured me that if it didn't really work out, we could send the intern home early. This was not ideal, but at least there was an escape hatch. I told Esha we would run the experiment.

Later that year, Wojciech Sankowski from Lodz, Poland, landed at Menlo for a six-month stay. He came in, contributed, learned a lot, and endeared himself to the team. As our first international intern, he was an excellent ambassador both for IAESTE and for his country. Our only disappointment was that his time with us was too short.

We were so gratified with the results of this experiment that we chose two interns the next year, for twelve months. This time we hosted Femi from Northern Ireland and Michael from Denmark. The following year, we requested four interns. Ever since, we have been bringing in four, five, or six interns each year. As of early 2013, we have had thirty-nine total IAESTE interns. The vast majority were wonderful additions to our team.

This experiment also provided us two unexpected, valuable results. When the new interns arrived, we were forced to practice onboarding new people even when the economy had slowed down. This was very healthy for us, since we couldn't get complacent and comfortable always having the same people around us. It also began to inform our ongoing desire for cognitive diversity. The IAESTE interns ensured that we wouldn't have only local grads employed at Menlo.

Experiment: Menlo Babies

Our most joyful experiment had nothing to do with software. In fact, it was a return to embracing the very human needs of our workers, in a way that is rejected almost out of hand by most companies today.

In 2007, Tracy, who had just recently joined Menlo, and her husband had their second child, Maggie. Tracy took about three months of paid maternity leave. She came into the office one day and let me know she was ready to come back to work, but Maggie was too young for day care and she didn't have anyone to babysit. She was stuck for an idea on how to make this work.

What happened next was a pivotal moment in my life as a manager, an entrepreneur, and a leader. As the next sentence began to form in my brain, I became aware of this silent screaming match happening in my head:

I know what you're about to say! Don't do it. It's against the rules. HR will hate you, silently screamed old manager Rich. New and improved manager Rich firmly retorted, *There are no rules about this here. We've never had an HR department. It's our company—we can do anything we want. Go away.*

"Bring Maggie in," I offered, not betraying the struggle I had just resolved in my own mind. "Bring Maggie in to work with you."

If only I'd had a camera. Tracy's face was a beautiful look of bewildered confusion. She starting questioning every element of this crazy idea. Did I mean every once in while or every day? If every day, did I mean that she was allowed to have her daughter with her at work all day? Then she looked around this big, wide, open room that is the Menlo Software Factory, where there are no walls, no cubes, no offices, no doors. "Where will I put her?" she asked.

"Put her in a bassinet on the floor next to wherever you happen to be working," I said. "She's not going anywhere." If we were going to run this experiment, I reasoned, we should be both serious and very open with it. It wasn't clear that this would be an easy experiment, but the potential for success was there.

"What if she makes a fuss?" she asked.

"Here? You'll never hear it. It's like a noisy restaurant all day. Besides, I remember raising my own kids. They loved noisy environments at her age."

"Yeah, but what if she really makes a fuss?" she persisted. I'm pretty sure she was thrilled by my idea but wanted to confirm just how much I'd thought this through (which admittedly wasn't much).

In response, I gave what might have been the most sanguine piece of management wisdom in my career to date: "Tracy, I trust you. You're the mom. I know how moms are. If there are problems, you'll do the right thing."

Maggie came in to work with Tracy almost every day for much of the next four months. She was a great addition to our culture, as she confirmed for us and the world that no experimental idea is too crazy to contemplate. Besides, Maggie's presence was joyful and made us all feel more real and human. For the most part, my optimism was confirmed. When Maggie did make noise, it was usually as squeals of delight in response to all the energy and activity in the room.

Of course, there were times when Maggie would cry and fuss, loudly, as is typical of any newborn. This is where my prediction failed to take into account the response of the team to having a baby in the room. It was seldom Tracy who had to rescue Maggie. The team would rush to declare, "It's my turn to hold Maggie." I would sometimes win these races. She brought delight to all of us and, in

Greg (and baby Ellie) and his pair partner, Kamil, work together at one station.

return, the entire Menlo village helped raise Maggie. We even learned that our clients would behave better when we brought Maggie to the meetings. Customers won't raise their voices or swear if there is a baby in the room.

After we ran the experiment with Maggie, we decided the babies could be integrated into the Menlo culture really well. Maggie, Solomon, and Lily were the first three babies. Solomon stayed until after his first birthday; we had to build a large playpen for him because he stayed until after he could walk. Since then, we've hosted Noel, Abigail, Kalina, and now Henry and Ellie, to round out the octet of Menlo babies so far. I've told all the Menlo parents that my goal is to give them a chance to see those precious firsts: the first time they turn over, sit up, smile, laugh—whatever it might be.

Having children in the office has forced us to run other small experiments in order to support a baby-friendly workforce. It has had unexpected results for our business dealings as well. One of my personal favorite stories that arose from this experiment involved Solomon, Christina's firstborn. One day I was holding Solomon, with Christina standing with her back to me about twenty feet away. I was waiting for a potential client to call. As the phone rang, Solomon began to fidget and make noise. Uh-oh. I had to get Christina's attention so I could give my undivided attention to the call—but I couldn't. The phone rang three times and was about to roll over to voice mail. I needed to make a command decision, so I picked up the phone, Solomon still in hand.

If you've ever had kids or been around them, you know there seems to be a special understanding that babies have about adults and telephones. They seem to implicitly understand that you are trapped by the phone and they can get away with pretty much anything when you have this object glued to your ear. I quickly realized I was in this classic trap within the first thirty seconds of my important call, so I figured I should just fess up.

"By the way, you are going to hear a baby in the background," I said to my new, important client.

"Oh, are you working at home today?" the caller asked.

"No, I'm at work," I responded rather matter-of-factly.

"Oh, you bring your child to work with you?" she asked, puzzled.

"It's not mine," I said, revealing the full scale of how weird this CEO really was.

"What do you mean?"

I explained our practice of allowing new parents to bring their babies in all day, every day.

"Oh, my gosh," the client declared emphatically. "I want to work with a company that thinks like you do."

I had never even considered the marketing effect the babies would have on our client relationships. But here it was—the baby's presence may have helped secure a new deal because the client responded positively to our willingness to think outside the box.

We've since won awards for our support of working moms and dads, including recognition for breastfeeding support. Our support extends to time for parents as well. There are usually extra time-off needs for well-baby checks, as well as time to stay at home with a sick child or attend a school or sports function as the kids get older. Our pairing system ensures we always have backups to anyone on the team who needs time off for personal needs.

Most who question the thinking of this particular experiment can't help but wonder about the liability of having babies around the office. But if you think about it, parents have been raising babies in far more dangerous environments than Menlo for millions of years, and we seem to be doing a pretty good job perpetuating the human race. Besides, in our scenario, Mom or Dad is with the child all day long. These children are wonderfully socialized by the time they leave Menlo.

Our babies experiment was a stepping-stone for running further experiments. We've since successfully hosted older children—and dogs!—as well. But, of course, babies and dogs in the workplace are not the sole point of these work/life experiments.

If you are the leader, your team watches you. Do you actually mean what you say? The team will continuously look for clues and inconsistencies in your message and your actions. If they find those inconsistencies, you'll soon witness a rise in fear. It doesn't take much fear to wipe out that *feel safe* culture, and suddenly you're commanding a *being safe* culture.

We look to embrace the life of each team member in whatever way makes sense for the business and the person. Not all of the experiments we run are as joy filled as the baby stories. These are the team members who had to care for a spouse or parent during a protracted illness, or worse. These events are personal and painful, but they happen in real life, and a company needs to be flexible and open enough to deal with them. Every organization needs to make room for the time or effort a person needs for his or her personal life, and the dividends of this effort are not measured in business terms.

The Reward Is in the Attempt

The experiments you run in the culture of *make mistakes faster* can and should be quick and inexpensive. That way, you won't be burdened by the sunk-cost thinking of "We can't afford to change this experiment if it isn't working as planned." Not all experiments work. Being able to accept this is where quietly confident leadership plays a role. Revel in the attempt and move on.

EIGHT

Growing Leaders, Not Bosses

A leader is best when people barely know he exists. When his work is done, his aim fulfilled, they will say: we did it ourselves.

—LAO-TZU

One late Friday afternoon before the Memorial Day weekend, Ian, one of our longtime programmers, was looking at code and noticed some unprofessional words being used. Nothing really awful or malicious, but they would have made a kindergarten teacher blush. He did a little digging and found a few more of these choice phrases. He recorded them and brought them to the project manager, who passed them to me. I immediately asked the team to gather in the training area. This was one of the most challenging "Hey, Menlo's" I have ever called.

I expressed my deep disappointment in what had been found and requested an all-hands-on-deck effort for the rest of that Friday afternoon to determine if this problem was pervasive or rare. We would need people to work that weekend in order to complete the review quickly and be back to regular operations by Tuesday. No one at Menlo ever expects to work on any weekend and certainly not the first holiday weekend of the summer. This was a painful and unprecedented request.

Ian raised his hand and volunteered without hesitation; Nick, his pair partner, did the same. Others joined in. It would have been easy for Ian to think his involvement ended at the discovery. Leadership means not only reinforcing core values when convenient, but also signing up for fixing the problem when those values have been compromised. It was particularly rewarding to see this happen with Ian; he had been with us for a long time as his late father, David, had introduced him to Menlo early in his career. His actions reminded me that leadership can come from anywhere.

Although it would have been quite easy to find the programmers who'd added these words, I was not going to ask for a witch hunt. Turning such an event into a finger-pointing exercise would have missed the opportunity for growth. At the moment when I could have defined an action plan, I paused and left an opening to allow others to lead. I hoped there would be team members stepping up to lead, and there were. No one had to tell them what to do.

It turned out the problem was not widespread and in no way affected the operation of the system. The following Tuesday, before Show & Tell, we let the client know what we had found and how we'd dealt with it. The client was disappointed, too, but thankful for our straightforward reporting and handling of the situation.

Ian's story is typical of how we are growing leaders at Menlo. Ian wasn't a boss. He didn't have a manager title, and yet he led this effort without being anointed or authorized to do so. The team followed his lead and was influenced by his caring. No, we have not completely eliminated positional authority or standard business titles such as CEO, COO, CFO, or manager. However, leadership at Menlo does not rest with a title or a position. Some leadership is situational. Some leadership grows through increasing influence based on respect and experience.

As I consider those at Menlo who lead most naturally, it is the people who are inclusive and respectful of others. These leaders exhibit a calm, patient, and quiet confidence. They exercise emotional control and allow those they are leading to make mistakes while ensuring they don't flounder. They are gentle, empathetic, trusting teachers. They have established themselves as leaders, in part, because of who they are and how they behave, and because we have created a culture that welcomes the courage and desire it takes to step outside yourself and your role and lead others. Menlonians don't need to request a position or promotion to assert their influence.

In our quest for joy, we have eliminated hierarchy. It's not easy, and some team members grapple with the freedom and responsibility of our leadership style. Others wish that we, the bosses, would just step in and declare how to do things. It would be faster in the short term, but we take a long-term view. Leadership is an art that is born out of skills that must be practiced. Those few of us who do have a title and positional authority must learn to look at every moment, whether difficult or important, as an opportunity to see whether a new leader is ready to step up and exercise his or her leadership skills. Perhaps some are born to lead, but we believe all are capable. In both cases, there must be a willingness and a desire to lead.

Let Your Team Lead Without You

We took on a project with a challenging client in the industry of helping others evaluate their corporate culture. These people had been in business for twenty years, quite successfully, and were well regarded in their field. They had, however, been stuck for a decade trying to bring a new product offering to market, one, if done right, that could allow them to grow the company tenfold. They had failed several times on their own and brought us in to help. We could quickly and obviously see where their own culture of fear was defeating their ability to perceive a problem. This blind spot also prevented them from discerning potential solutions.

Our clients were getting frustrated with our systematic approach, as they were expecting simpler answers than we were offering. They began exporting fear all the way back to us. The most tangible evidence of fear was the complete unproductivity of the meetings we had with them. No decisions were being made, and they would delay setting up the next meeting. Whenever their mostly absent founder spoke at one of these meetings, everyone else on their team would go silent for the remainder of the time. The Menlo team approached me in the hope that I would join the next client meeting and get things back on track.

I chose not to join the meeting. Instead, I assured the team that they were safe and encouraged them to confidently reinforce our values with our client. Don't get me wrong—staying away from this meeting was difficult for me. Every bone in my body wanted to be in that meeting so I could exercise every bit of my talent for mending a breaking relationship.

The team members, knowing I trusted them to represent our values, ran the next meeting on their own. It went well. Michelle P. told me later that it was comforting to hear, just one more time, that I trusted them and that they had the authority to handle these situations. We may sometimes have to fire a client, or they may beat us to the punch, but our people know it will never be seen as their fault. This is not to say that we're fully blameless or that we transfer all the fault to the client; it's important to make the client feel honored throughout this process.

Often the most important leadership moments occur when we lead by stepping out of the way and letting the team take over. Accept that something has gone in a direction that you did not expect and perhaps don't even fully support. You then must have the patience to see that the team is learning from this experience and that its own leadership talents are developing in these moments of mistake making.

Be Vulnerable

As a leader, your team is constantly watching you and actively looking for chinks in the armor. They so want to believe you—and believe in you—but others have disappointed them in the past, so they are wary. You have also disappointed them. I know I have disappointed my team, but I try to keep it to less than one disappointment a week.

I don't have all the answers. Sometimes I just wish I had the right questions. However, I am still willing to make decisions. And I don't want to be the decision-making bottleneck, either. Sometimes my answer has to be "I trust you to make a good decision." The more joyful path is to create a culture in which you aren't even asked to make a call. Someone will simply catch you later and say, "By the way, we made an important decision today. Let me know if you want any of the details."

The hardest part of leadership is remembering that you are just as fallible as anyone else in the organization. Part of that fallibility is expressed in how your entire organization works, or doesn't work, at any given moment. In Jim Collins's *Good to Great*, he describes the humility of great leaders, those he calls "Level 5" leaders. I'm sure I fail this test almost every time. It's hard to get the attention we do and stay humble, but it's so important. Fortunately, I have enough people around me that care enough to bring me back down to earth on a regular basis: my business partners, key members of the team, and my family.

A big part of vulnerability and humility is to hear over and over again that this thing you love so much and believe in to your core is not perfect. We have the same problems as any other organization. Almost every single one. We have problems with team members not getting along with one another; we have challenges when the founders don't always agree on the future direction of the company, or when the team disagrees on whether we are doing the right thing for a client or whether we are sticking to our guns when we need to. What I hope is that we've created a system that exposes these problems sooner, so that we can deal with them while they are still small.

My goal in all of these small defeats is to remember how special this thing is that we've created and to remind our team that, despite all of our challenges, we still have something many others do not: a culture everyone on the team wants to live to see another day, another month, another year, another decade. That is a very powerful force.

Part of the vulnerability of not having all the answers is the humility to share your ideas with your team before they are fully formulated. These ideas are often like babies. We believe they are beautiful, but often the beauty is seen in our perfectly imagined hopes for the future rather than in the reality of the moment.

In 2011, I drafted a personal vision for what I thought Menlo would look like in June 2018. Much of it was very personal, as it outlined how Menlo would have an impact on my life and that of my family. It even mentioned how many grandchildren I would have by then, even though I had none in 2011. The vision included outside-of-work elements, such as a vacation home in northern Michigan, which would also be used for annual Menlo retreats. I wrote in great detail what the business would look like in annual revenues, how many employees we'd have, and what impact we would be having in the community. I also envisioned having launched my third book, *Inspired: The Joy of Entrepreneurship*, which was a bold pronouncement, as I had yet to start writing my first book.

After I finished writing my personal vision, I shared it with the entire team so they could see what I was thinking about our future, and mine. If I were successful in gaining followers of what I was outlining, this would be the first step in moving from a personal vision to one shared by the whole team. While I was describing something seven years in the future, the implications of this vision would mean we'd have to start changing soon. In short, I was sharing an important personal aspiration with those who could help me get there. What if they didn't like it? What if they didn't want to join me? It was a vulnerable moment, but I knew if some version of this were ever to become a *shared* vision, it would have to be, well, shared. By sharing your ideas while still at the conceptual phase, you are letting go of the feeling "This is my idea—isn't it great? Aren't I smart?" This is particularly difficult for engineers like me, whose self-worth is often derived from being seen as the smartest one in the room. The power in this, though, is that most ideas can be made so much better with more minds involved.

The team didn't quite know how to embrace this vision. I'm sure there were parts they agreed with and other parts they weren't sure about. It probably wasn't clear how it would affect them. For example, one part of the vision was to be an incubator of new companies. Well, that can be a lot of work, and if you aren't particularly interested in that kind of thing, how do you participate?

If the vision isn't shared, then no one has a chance of learning whether he or she fits or not. Drilling down on your vision also gives others a chance to respond and participate in improving it. During this period, the personal vision of an individual evolves into the shared vision of a team.

While this is a rare example, as I'm not in the habit of sharing seven-year visions very often, it is representative of a style of leadership that says, "I'm not smart enough to have all the answers, and I'm willing to accept that my personal view may not be the right one." In short, "I need your help."

Encourage New Leaders

Nate, one of our software developers, has been with the company for a few years. He and I have had an ongoing discussion about how exciting our career start was because we were blessed to be exposed to programming at a young age. We lament that not all middle school and high school students, even in a college town like Ann Arbor, have a similar opportunity.

Nate gathered a few of his friends from outside Menlo and started working on the curriculum and equipment for a software summer camp for third graders to eighth graders. The plan was to have them come in to Menlo a couple of days a week during the summer to hack the computer game Minecraft, using the Python programming language. He started running experimental camps with children of Menlonians just to see whether they liked it. They loved it. Glenn, one of our clients, came in for Show & Tell and saw the kids at work in the training area and asked what was going on. When we explained the experiment to him, he immediately asked if he could sign up his eleven-year-old for the camp.

If members of your team show a spark of inspiration or passion, support them. Feed their dream and encourage them as they pursue it. It's the best way to support someone's leadership development.

John M. started out as a programmer at Menlo and quickly gained the trust of the team. He was good at programming and a great pair partner. During a period of high demand for our High-Tech Anthropology services, John was recruited to try his hand at being an HTA. He accepted the challenge without hesitation and excelled, working as an HTA for quite some time. The developers valued John, and complained that he had been stolen away from them.

John then asked if he could try his hand at project management. Sure—why not? When project manager Lisa H. took a long vacation with her husband, John was able to step in and lead as a PM in her absence. He did a great job, and upon Lisa's return, stepped back into a programming role.

We appreciate the flexibility that someone like John can provide us. His willingness to enthusiastically try new things grew his natural leadership ability. He now has a well-rounded appreciation of the challenges other roles on the team face and can shift into a leadership mode when the occasion calls for it.

One of the most important roles James and I have at Menlo is to encourage and support leadership development in others. This isn't as easy as it sounds because there can be times when the disconnect between our vision of leadership and a budding leader is quite wide. Society teaches us that leaders tell and followers listen. We don't believe in that style of leadership at Menlo. We seek to grow leaders who act like gentle teachers rather than schoolyard bullies.

New leaders at Menlo must experience *feeling safe* as they test their emerging leadership skills. If not, their own fear is easily exported to others, and that results in the overall theft of our creativity, our imagination, and our joy.

It would be easy to say that fear comes only from within the organization or from the leadership. In business, fear can come from anywhere: competitors, bad hires, bad days with good hires, economic turmoil, bad checks, unpaid invoices, market shifts, the evening news, gossip. Calm, thoughtful leadership can go a long way to help alleviate the fear that does occur.

One classic fear scenario that has been repeated often at Menlo is when the customer brings the fear into the room. We all carry around this age-old mantra in our heads: *The customer is always right.*

No, they're not. In fact, the customer is *seldom* right. If the customer was always right, why would they need us? This is particularly true for a firm like ours, where our clients are asking us to create an entirely new product within their domain, often a domain in which they are experts and dominant players. They are looking for something new, compelling, and competitive. Our difficulty rarely lies in coming up with something innovative and delightful; rather, it is in the resistance to change that exists within their own organization.

Thus, we have to fight for what we believe is right from our experience, talent, and expertise. These healthy fights need to be based on what we discover in our observations and iterative testing of design. Our customers often want what we can do, unless and until we disagree with them. This constructive conflict is hard and important and is at the very heart of where we deliver all of our value.

However, my team understands that by taking a firm stand based on our beliefs, expertise, and experience, our customers might actually fire us. If a client fires us, they might even go so far as to not pay one or more of our outstanding invoices. The risk of standing on our beliefs can have a very real cost for all of us.

In other cases, we might have to fire a client. It's not unheard of for Menlo to let go of a client. A few years ago, we had a significant client with whom we felt a real cultural incompatibility. After trying every approach we could to get them on the track we thought was best for them, we both conceded the fit was just not there and built a thoughtful transition plan so that they would not be left in the lurch.

While such a decision meant lower revenue, less profit, and slower growth, it may be the most important kind of decision I can make to reinforce our culture. It's never easy. It's never straightforward. As with letting staff go, we must do this with dignity and respect. I have to say that the most gratifying aspect of successfully transitioning this client's work away from Menlo is that we are still friends with the champions of that project. They still reach out to us every now and then for advice. We even helped them recruit the necessary staff to fill the gap created by our parting ways.

Your team and my team watch and listen, looking, feeling, observing their leaders during difficult stretches. This is where the intentionally joyful culture rubber meets the road.

End Chaos, Eliminate Ambiguity

Do the simplest thing that can possibly work.

—KENT BECK, *Extreme Programming Explained*

In my old chaotic VP life at Interface Systems, before the Java Factory began, I would be invited to the boardroom and asked to make a quarterly "state of the department" presentation for the R&D team I was leading. I would present the last quarter's goals, the progress we had made, note what we had worked on outside of the plan, provide an updated plan with new goals, and reflect on how those goals related to the rest of the company. At the end of the presentation, my executive peers would usually voice some disappointment about how my team had been pulled off track from the previous quarter's stated goals by unexpected tasks. They would then offer general encouragement about the updated plan, along with some fear-based remarks about how important it would be to stay on track, as all of their department plans were depending on my team's execution.

I couldn't get more than twenty feet from the boardroom when some VP or product manager would pull me aside and say something like, "Great presentation, Rich, but there's just one more thing I want to talk with you about. I need Aaron to do a special update for a customer. If he can get it done by Friday, we can close the deal." Scope creep in action.

Of course, in my earliest days, I wanted to be the helpful Boy Scout, so I would somehow figure out a way to get that work done.

I came to learn that this hallway project management approach did not make my life any better. It was also hell for any programmer. Each quarter, the reported list of things we actually worked on had almost no relationship to my previously stated goals. So I tried getting everyone to agree to the stated goals in the meeting, in the presence of the CEO. That unified agreement quickly ended out in the hallway, where the real project management work was being done.

Eventually, my executive peers discovered they really didn't need me in these casual discussions. Much of the re-prioritization of my team's work was now being concluded in the bowling and golf leagues or during after-work drinks. I'd come in one morning and find my programmers busily working on an assignment I'd never given them.

No matter how the current assignments got into my team's queue, I now owned all of them. My peers were now demanding updates, as everything was way behind. They wanted to know when these new priorities were going to be done. In general, my developers, who were not very practiced at estimating, reverted to a time-honored estimation standard —the not very useful "a couple of days."

When I'd hear one of my team members say it would take "a couple of days" to work on an assignment, I'd think, *Cool, I have that person busy for a couple of days.* After three days, I'd check in and ask how it was going. I'd usually hear a pretty enthusiastic "Great!" That felt good until I'd check on the aforementioned two-day task. I'd find out that the small project was exactly as I'd left it. This was usually followed by an explanation that some unexpected interruptions, usually a hot customer support issue, had taken their attention away from their "couple of days" project.

This cycle continued for another two or three rounds before I'd start asking for a more serious appraisal. That's when I'd hear that the work was just a little harder than my developer had originally anticipated, and now he had a better understanding of the project. He updated his estimate to two weeks. Now I had a serious estimate.

This was usually followed by a couple of rounds of saying he was two weeks away from completion.

Finally, the programmer would revert to the estimate that kept all the hounds at bay: three months. This last estimate achieves nirvana; no one will bother him for three months.

This entire system may have actually had a chance of working, had it not been for one glaring problem: the rest of the organization wasn't a team but rather a bunch of competing fiefdoms. Each earl of a fiefdom really cared only about his projects getting done. There was little I could do to provide visibility into total workload, as no one really knew everything that was going on, including me.

This was compounded by the quality issues that arose when tired programmers pulling all-nighters were trying to meet the personal commitments they'd made during those after-work conversations. Our support line rang off the hook with trouble, and I kept having to dedicate a greater and greater percentage of my team's efforts to firefighting. I'd then get hammered for having a team that produced crappy quality. This was chaos compounded and multiplied by ambiguity.

I am thrilled to report we have none of these problems at Menlo and haven't in our entire history. While many of our visitors could easily claim three hundred calls per day on their trouble line, we haven't had more than a handful of emergency calls in our twelve-year history. The last time my team remembers a true "drop everything" style client emergency was in 2004.

The reason we avoid chaos at Menlo is simple: we operate with clarity, simplicity, and predictability.

Write It Down

One of the strongest rules at Menlo is that nothing gets done on a client project unless it is first handwritten on a 5½-by-8½-inch

Writing out a story card by hand.

index card. The card has a simple structure: it's labeled with the project code name, a serial number for the card (starting at 001 for each project and counting up from there), a brief title, and a short description that defines how the work of the card will affect the resulting software. All story cards must be signed and dated by the people who wrote the cards. Any team member can write a card. While atypical, cards could be written by team members who are not even assigned to the project. They could be written by clients.

Once the card is completed, it is then given to the project managers. The project managers have an index card box on their tables where these new cards are collected. In our system, the project manager assigns the story card's sequence number to avoid duplicates.

This simple tool destroys the possibility of hallway project management. If it isn't written down, then a newly stated requirement is just a conversation with no possibility of action. Everyone at Menlo, including our customers, is very clear on this point.

No Work Without Estimation

Just because a card is written doesn't mean it will ever be worked on. This is why it's important, as in every culture, for there to be a clear pattern of decision making to determine how long a given task will take.

At Menlo, each story card must be estimated by the people who do the work. This happens in our weekly estimation session. Once estimated, a photocopy of the estimated card is folded to a size relative to the estimate as defined in the Planning Origami technique described earlier. The folded cards are then laid on top of a planning table alongside empty planning sheets that correspond to the client's weekly budget, one sheet for each pair of resources budgeted for this client's project. Each planning sheet is inscribed with an empty box that is sized to hold thirty-two hours of folded story cards. We set aside the other eight hours for the standard work of our process: two hours for weekly estimation, two hours for weekly Show & Tell with the client, two hours for the team's weekly project kickoff conversation, one hour for daily standup (twelve minutes per day, five days a week), and one hour for other team communication.

Declare What You Are Doing and Not Doing

After we've done our estimation work internally, our client comes in and reviews the estimated cards and prioritizes them through the planning game process. If a card makes it onto one of the planning sheets for the week, the client has just authorized us to work on the card and bill them for that work.

Perhaps even more important, if a card is left on the table and not moved to a planning sheet, it is perfectly clear to everyone that this work is not authorized and will not be worked on. This simple visual system makes some tour visitors laugh at just how clear and adoptable this is. Basically, they have just witnessed the destruction of their own tortured life of hallway project management. In corporate hallways around the world many decisions are made in sidebar conversations. These decisions are typically never recorded. Likewise, these new decisions are typically never evaluated for the effect they might have on all other existing priorities. They are just added to the list of things that must be done. This is where the seeds of a coming "death march" are planted.

Our clients know they can't come in the next week and ask why a certain card didn't get worked on. If they wanted it in the plan, they put the card on the planning sheet. It's that simple; it's that clear. I have yet to find another project management system that shows what you have decided to do and what not to do as clearly as ours.

Record Your Decisions

When the planning decisions have been made, our project managers then apply formal "change control" so that we can all be assured that decisions are properly recorded for future status reporting. We use 3M's Scotch Transparent Tape technology to tape the folded cards to the planning sheets. Very high-tech.

It is now clear to everyone who looks at the sheet—from programmers to High-Tech Anthropologists to the clients to anyone on the team—what decisions have been made about the work to be done on the project. We make a PDF of the planning sheet for our files and e-mail it to our clients so that they, too, have a record of their decisions.

Unambiguously Assign Work

Once the client selects the cards they want us to work on in a given week, the project manager will pin a copy of the card to the wall, underneath an index card header with names of the Menlo pair assigned to work on the task.

This is the only way work gets authorized at Menlo. No one is confused. We know exactly who is assigned to a story card. Anyone can go over to the wall and see what Corey and Wes are working on this week.

Compare this to decision making and assignments in most of the business world, perhaps the world you work in every day. If it is anything like my old chaotic life, a lot of these assignments are meted out in meetings. There is a whiteboard, a flip chart, and notebooks (paper and electronic). One person leads the meeting and the discussion is meandering and broad. You may spend some time on pursuing and advocating work items or arguing about who gets what assignment and when a certain deadline is. When the conference room booking time nears its end, the meeting's leader will say, "Okay, so we are all on the same page, right?"

What page exactly? The whiteboard in front of the room, or one of the six scribbled flip chart pages? A page in someone's notebook with their interpretation of the last hour's discussion or a virtual page on someone's laptop with their totally different take on the meeting? If I caught everyone individually five minutes after the meeting and asked each one what had been decided, would I get even two answers that matched? If I asked what had been decided *against*, would anyone even know what I meant? And when exactly are people going to start working on everything that was discussed in the meeting, and who exactly is going to work on it?

At Menlo there is zero ambiguity in the decision making as our simple paper-based tools answer all of these questions without extra effort.

Simple Systems for Complex Projects

We don't use these simple tools only to manage assignments one week at a time or just over the short term. Multiyear, multimillion-dollar mission-critical projects are planned, organized, and tracked in an identical way. Even our most complex systems, those that adhere to federal agency guidelines, get the story card treatment.

We have one project at Menlo that we've been working on for over seven years with nearly two hundred thousand hours of effort. The total number of story cards is approaching ten thousand. Some marvel that we can keep track of this many cards in a paper-based system. First of all, we do have an Excel spreadsheet with each card and title cataloged as well as the disposition of the card. Fewer than a few hundred of these cards are active in any given time period. Most of the cards are simply historical. Regardless, we've never found an electronic system that does a better job of keeping track of our projects than our story card system.

This is not to say we're unaware of disaster preparedness. Menlo does rely on simple high-technology answers as safeguards against the unexpected, such as fire or flood. Every photocopier we have used over the years can read and image a stack of index cards. These PDF images are stored on our servers and are e-mailed to our clients weekly. We also carry backup disk packs to an off-site storage location in a local bank vault.

Hot Pink Decisions

In the earliest days of the Java Factory at Interface Systems, the paper-based planning system was working reasonably well, but I still had this haunted feeling that we were spending way too much time on the old products. This was constraining my team's ability to complete the new products that the market and my executive peers were demanding.

I shared these concerns with CEO Bob Nero, who would try to reassure me by saying he knew I was up to the challenge of figuring all of this out. I clearly wasn't communicating in a way that was letting him know exactly how big a problem this actually was. Bob was a busy guy, and it was hard for him to see the level of detail that would have frightened him enough to significantly influence priorities.

James had the idea of copying any old project maintenance story cards onto hot pink paper; all the other story cards were white. Now when planning was complete, it was very obvious that maintenance work on aging products was consuming more than 50 percent of my team's capacity. You needed only to glance at the planning game sheets to see the amount of pink paper.

One afternoon, Bob walked into the Java Factory to check in with me and noticed the hot pink cards easily chewing up half the planning sheets. They clearly got his attention and he asked what the hot pink signified. I told him those hot pink cards represented the maintenance work I was worried about.

"What? That's more than half your team!" Bob lamented.

At that point, he stepped up to the table and grabbed a random pink card to see what my team was being asked to work on. Ed, one of our sales guys, had authorized this work. Bob summoned Ed out to the Java Factory and demanded to know why we were working on this particular story card. What value did it have to the bottom line? Ed informed him that if we got that done, then IBM would place an order for our product. Bob handed the folded story card to Ed and instructed him to go get a conditional purchase order from IBM saying that if we got the feature done, IBM would commit to buying the enhanced product. The order never arrived, so we yanked the pink card.

Bob was quite pleased and looked at the empty spot on the planning sheet and said, "Rich, let's make sure we get a white card in that empty spot."

Simple, clear, and unambiguous tools create opportunity for meaningful conversations that aren't confounded by technology. Now we need to make sure every opportunity exists for those conversations to occur; we cannot wait for Monday morning status meetings. Those *conversations* have to be given a chance to occur exactly when they need to—and our space, our culture, and our process make sure that is the case.

Once the decisions are made and declared unambiguously, we must establish the practices that will ensure that the work will be done with rigor and discipline. Only then will you have the chance to produce the type of quality that yields the pride of a job well done.

Rigor, Discipline, Quality

All anyone asks for is a chance to work with pride.

—W. EDWARDS DEMING

In Menlo's early years, we worked on the patient information system for a transplant surgery unit within a large regional hospital. Several months into the project, the hospital's contract administrator learned we were working in pairs. We never hide that aspect of our work; she just hadn't paid close attention to the details of the work we were doing. I was summoned to her office at the hospital.

"I understand your people work two to a computer."

"Yes, that's correct. It's a technique called pair programming—"

She abruptly cut me off. She demanded to know whether she had to pay for both of these people. Yes, I assured her, every person working on the effort was being billed to her project. Stop working this way, she ordered me—but then asked why we worked this way.

We worked *this way*, in pairs, for the same reason her hospital worked in pairs, I said. My daughter had just undergone major surgery for a severe bone break she'd suffered from a fall during a soccer game. The surgeons showed up as a pair to introduce themselves before surgery. Same for the pair of anesthesiologists and the nursing pair.

"Your daughter's life is at stake. That's why we do that," she replied, trying to dress me down.

For the system we were working on for her organization, I explained, if we got something as basic as the tissue type wrong for a transplant, we might kill the patient. We believe that people's lives or at least livelihoods can be at stake if we don't have that type of discipline and risk checking as well. The quality of work done in pairing is as important to our industry as it is to hers.

The question of pairing programmers never came up again.

In 2012, I read a story about how one of Knight Capital's most talented and senior technical people had made a mistake upgrading server software that controlled the company's automated trading system. During the next forty-five minutes, that simple technical mistake led to $7 billion of erroneous stock trades that cost Knight Capital over $400 million. I can't say that pairing would have prevented this error, but it might have made it a lot less likely. Software is now in everything. It controls your car, commercial airliners, nuclear reactors, banking systems, stock trading systems, coffee shops. Software errors can cause great risk to humans, to companies, and to economies. The same magnitude of risk exists in other industries, perhaps in yours. An incorrect patent application can cost a company a great deal of money years down the road. A police officer's split-second decision can mean life or death for himself or an innocent bystander.

Pairing increases quality and attention to detail particularly in cases of pressure, stress, and fatigue. The next time you step onto a commercial airliner, ask yourself how it would feel if you peeked into the cockpit and saw only one pilot. Imagine the captain then came on the intercom and explained that his copilot had called in sick today and thus he was going to be flying solo. He further explained that, despite the difficult weather at the destination and the fact that we was up all night with his sick child, he was confident there wouldn't be any problem. I'll just bet those seated in the exit rows would immediately figure out how to open the emergency doors.

Wash Your Hands

One of the saddest versions of failed attempts to introduce new rigorous quality practices occurred in the Vienna General Hospital in the mid 1800s. As part of his research, Ignaz Philipp Semmelweis discovered a vital connection between hand washing and survival rates for the mothers who gave birth there. Interns and their teachers regularly proceeded from working on cadavers to assisting on births, without washing their hands. Semmelweis attempted to establish a regular pattern of hand washing to ensure the mothers didn't die from infection. He was unsuccessful in his pursuit, as the doctors insisted it wasn't a problem and they were too busy and important for such foolishness.

The relentless criticism that Semmelweis encountered broke his spirit. By 1865, he was depressed and suffering from a host of neural complaints. He was ultimately committed to an asylum and died soon thereafter at the age of forty-seven. Of course, we now know, tragically, that Semmelweis was right. Rigor and discipline could have saved so many lives in his industry. His attention to quality was ignored in his time but is standard in our health care systems today.

You must seek and rigorously apply your industry's version of hand washing. What quality practices can you introduce that uphold your values and keep your team safe and organized? For pilots, it became checklists; for restaurants, hand washing and hairnets; for blood banks, exhaustive questionnaires and systematic screening; for pharmacy chains, automated drug interaction warnings; and for the food industry, expiration dates.

What methods, what practices, what disciplines will be required to give us the best chance of working with pride? In other words, *how* exactly will we do our work?

Many who come in to visit Menlo see the fun and frivolity of our whimsically irreverent workplace. This setting could give the impression that we have a laissez-faire attitude toward workmanship or quality. That couldn't be further from the truth. The rigor and discipline that exist just an inch below the surface of what you see at Menlo has led to unprecedented quality in our products.

Whether you manage a deli, a hospital, an airline, a fire department, an automobile manufacturer, a daring circus, a patent practice, or a software company, the quality effect of rigor and discipline is of paramount importance. What can we do to ensure we get a chance to work with the pride that emanates from knowing you did the best job you could?

Heroes Rely on Risky Heroics, Great Teams Rely on Discipline

Alongside all the practices that contribute to quality at Menlo is the upward spiral of morale that comes from knowing you are operating within an environment where it is safe and respected to do good work.

Rigor and discipline are hard, and it's always easy to say, "Tomorrow I will do better." Tomorrow never comes—it is the actions we take today that make all the difference. If you can get your entire team into a disciplined routine of applying a rigorous approach you all believe in, and the effects become noticeable, morale soars even if the rigor is difficult. It is in these moments of rigor that the seeds of joy are planted. When your team enjoys the fruits of their labor, there will be an undeniable satisfaction that boosts morale and gets everyone ready to do it all again.

One such rigor for us is that our programmers must write automated unit tests *before* they write the code to be tested. Most programmers just want to get down to writing the code and, believing they did a good job, they convince themselves that writing an automated test for the code is unnecessary. It would be so easy to fall out of this habit, but it is so crucial to the level of quality we aspire to in the code. However, our discipline demands that we write the test before we write the code, and it guarantees we will do it every time.

In 1980, I began my first Ann Arbor programming job at Manufacturing Data Systems, Inc. (MDSI), one of the highest-flying tech firms in the history of the town. I was still in school at Michigan, so this was a part-time job until I graduated. At MDSI, I was surrounded by great people, including Larry Page's mom, Gloria, who was a programmer there, as was Thomas Knoll, who would go on to write Photoshop.

These were heady times in our industry, and MDSI had started a wonderful intern onboarding process the summer I joined. They taught us some disciplined coding standards that I recall to this day. One of the most unusual, but exciting, was something that today is called "test-driven design." In simple terms, it means that the programmers write automated tests for the code they are about to write, then they write the code, and finally they run the tests to make sure the code passes.

The effect on quality is unparalleled. This rigor ensures that silly human mistakes are caught automatically without having to remember all the little things that can go wrong. Think of this like having an auto mechanic who lives in your garage at home. Every night while you are sleeping, this tireless worker is checking tire pressure, steering linkage, brake linings, oil quality, the gas tank, air filter quality, window visibility, electrical systems, and making sure that every little nut and bolt is properly secured and in tip-top shape. Your car would probably last a million miles with this attention, but it's more important than that. Let's say that your drive to work was fifty miles through the freezing tundra with no cell phone service, and any mechanical breakdown would likely end in your freezing to death before help could arrive. You get the picture.

After completing this summer intern onboarding program at MDSI, I was given my departmental assignment and was duly instructed by my new boss to forget about that test-driven design approach, because we had real work to do. I wouldn't get another peek at this method until Kent Beck and Martin Fowler reintroduced the concept to the programming world in 2000 in the book *Refactoring.*

The rigorous application of an automated unit testing framework at Menlo is one of the strongest technical disciplines of our shared belief system. New programmers being onboarded are taught this approach by their pair partner. Quality soars, morale soars, and productivity soars, because we can move ahead faster with the confidence that we are not breaking things that have worked in the past. The tests are there to help us catch those mistakes.

Zingerman's deli has its own version of systematic quality testing. Each order is read back to the customer at every interaction. When you place your order, your order taker reads it back to you for confirmation. When you pay for your order, the cashier also does a read back. When the order is delivered to your table, the order is read back to you to confirm you're getting the right meal. Everyone at Zingerman's does this, every time. Can you imagine how much goodwill this creates with their customers? It doesn't improve the quality of the food itself (there are different processes for that), but it keeps the customer's experience at the highest level possible. It is easy to overlook obvious answers to serious quality issues.

Ensuring That Each Little Piece Is Right Still Doesn't Mean the Whole System Works

Another classic problem, particularly for software teams, is that systems are put together by lots of people, each working on his or her own little disconnected piece. Somewhere near the end of the project, the sparks start flying when all the pieces are finally put together. This integration usually becomes a late-stage project disaster never anticipated in any project plan. Nontechnical executives can't even comprehend what has just occurred on their multimillion-dollar mission-critical project.

To avoid this late-stage integration crunch, our entire team at Menlo checks to see whether their work actually fits together by continuously integrating the parts they are working on. There is never any late-stage surprise. If there are problems that result from integrating the work, we find these problems while we still have time and budget to deal with it. When this integration effort occurs only at the very end of a project, most software teams don't survive the inevitable late-stage disaster. Executives cancel the project and break up the team. While I don't know the inside story of that Ford Everest project that cost $400 million by the time it was canceled, I can easily imagine that integration issues were a factor. Tens of billions of dollars in our industry are wasted every year on projects that never see the light of day.

A live musical has similar integration challenges. During the weeks leading up to opening night, the orchestra works on the musical scores while the actors practice their songs and their lines. Dance troupes work on their choreography while stagehands, lighting crews, and other support staff go through crucial behind-the-scenes details. You can surely picture the disaster that would occur if the first fully integrated performance happened when the curtain rose on the evening of the first performance. Every individual might perform flawlessly, but the audience would see chaos. Seasoned directors know better. They continually do small integrations every step of the way to work through the flaws that aren't obvious until all are on the stage at the same time.

Teamwork and the trust necessary to carry out and complete the combined effort of an entire team require the discipline of systematic coordination. Until that level of discipline and rigor is established, the only way things will actually get done is through the heroic effort of a few individuals and we've already witnessed what happens to a culture that places all its bets on heroes and towers of knowledge.

Deliver Tangible Results Frequently

The best way we know to constantly test our system for weaknesses is to share our work with our clients. We let them into our testing and integration processes and let them experiment with our work at many stages so that they can witness our quality firsthand as we develop it.

Each week after Show & Tell, we send our client home with a CD or DVD of their fully integrated system so that they have the opportunity to more deeply explore what we have completed thus far. This is further confirmation that our integration work is, well, working. The point of this weekly delivery is to simply and practically reinforce our notion that PowerPoint, status reports, stage gate committee reviews, and so forth are no substitute for delivering working software. We're disciplined to deliver this material after every Show & Tell.

Anyone who has ever had a custom home built will tell you how they periodically visit the work site to check in on progress—some as often as daily. Are they experts in construction, carpentry, block laying, or plumbing? Of course not. They go to see the work because there is no verbal or written substitute for actually walking through the home, standing in an almost-finished kitchen where their family will eventually gather, or getting to know the view from the window looking over the backyard pond. Humans like to see, feel, and touch things they have a stake in. Reading a status report, watching a PowerPoint slide deck, or looking over a Gantt chart cannot replace the visceral response to walking through a house under construction or touching working software under development.

Sports teams have routines they go through to establish rigor and discipline. The best teams are dedicated to these routines, not just with their bodies but with their souls. The mediocre pay lip service to rigorous routines; they go through the motions, but they don't believe. The difference can be seen in the standings and can be felt on the field and up in the stands. For the very best, there are pride, honor, excitement, and energy that come from long-standing rigorous and disciplined traditions that well-told stories are made from.

Rigor and discipline and the quality that results reinforce your organization's definition of "why" you exist, a concept so elegantly explored by Simon Sinek in his book *Start with Why*. As Sinek explains, all organizations know what they do, some even know how they do it, but surprisingly few know why they do what they do. Your company's *why* goes straight to your purpose, your mission, and what you believe. If you can get to that level of quality, you can then achieve what most organizations believe is the ultimate goal: long-term sustainability of a culture and an organization.

ELEVEN

Sustainability and Flexibility

We cannot hope to create a sustainable culture with any but sustainable souls.

—DERRICK JENSEN,
Endgame, Vol. 1: The Problem of Civilization

There is so much talk today about sustainability. We vigorously debate the ecology of the planet, conservation of energy resources, health of ecosystems, protection of species, preservation of historic buildings, the revitalization of urban cores, conservation of sensitive habitats, and on and on.

I would like to bring a new sustainability topic to the table: *sustaining the humans who work for us.*

Consider the typical vacation preparation for so many employees: Laptop: check. Cell phone: check. VPN software properly configured: check. Our family, and particularly our children, then see us on the beach with a laptop or at dinner checking our e-mail. What message are we sending to our families when our work and home lives are barely distinguishable?

We take the *business value of joy* at Menlo very seriously. This is sometimes interpreted as some namby-pamby, People's Republic of Ann Arbor type of joy, but that couldn't be further from the truth. We are concerned with serious, entrepreneurial business value. When you work on projects that last years and consume hundreds of thousands of hours of effort, it would be foolish to approach this lightly. If we burn out our team two years into a seven-year project, they will still keep coming to work every day—they just won't bring their brains with them.

What Most Count as Workplace Flexibility Is Inhumane

Menlo has won the Alfred P. Sloan Award for Business Excellence in Workplace Flexibility seven times. One year, we received the highest overall score in the nation from the Sloan award, a research-based initiative by the When Work Works partnership between the Families and Work Institute and the Society for Human Resource Management. Yet despite our high scores and annual awards, we don't offer wild, flexible work hours, telecommuting, or work-from-home options. So why are we recognized for our workplace flexibility?

Employers often believe they are being flexible when they offer their team company cell phones, laptops, and secure VPN connections. What they're really saying is, "We expect you to be available twenty-four/seven, even on vacation." What flexibility is there in being on call every minute of every day? Companies that offer barbershops, on-site meals, and in-office doctors, dentists, and child care make it quite clear that once you get to the office, you are expected to stay. Many remote work arrangements are accompanied by an HR rules committee that is always trying to determine whether there is actually productive work being done.

So much for work/life balance. Try to hang out sometime in the offices that have Foosball tables, Ping-Pong tables, game stations, massage chairs, and workout rooms—and see how much these amenities are actually used. I once toured a small company that had a wonderful workout room. As we walked through it, I asked my guide whether the gym got a lot of use. He said that exercising on company time was frowned upon by the CEO, especially if you wanted to get ahead in the organization. No wonder the room looked great—everything was basically brand-new and never used.

We need every ounce of our team's creative capacity every minute of every day. If they are sick, tired, yearning for vacation or just some time to tend the garden at home or to take care of a loved one, they won't be present when they are at work. I don't know any other way to do this other than respect the whole lives of our team members. They deserve that from me and our company. At the end of a career, I don't want employees to lament the time they have spent at work away from family, or to realize that the work they delivered to the world was substandard, perhaps not ever delivered at all, or possibly universally hated by the people who used it.

At Menlo, we know the people who work the smartest and most conscientiously—who produce the best results for our clients—are people who know when to work and when to rest.

From Lisa H.:

In a few weeks, my husband and I will be leaving for a two-month vacation, and I can promise you that I won't be reading or responding to any work e-mails, and that expectation is embraced by our culture. To prepare for being gone, I have been pairing with Emily, one of our other project managers. Because we have been pairing, she is now prepared to take over these projects while I'm gone, and our clients know to contact her instead of me with any questions. The project manager role has been the one role at Menlo that hasn't had a strong pairing history. No longer. Once I'm back from my vacation, our plan is to continue project manager pairing on this project and others to avoid creating towers of knowledge again.

I am now free to enjoy my vacation and not think of work while I'm gone. This will allow me to come back to work refreshed and energized. I appreciate that Menlo lets my vacation truly be a vacation.

Choose a Sustainable Work Pace

We work forty-hour workweeks. That's Monday to Friday and never on weekends. We choose forty because we believe it is sustainable in the long run for most people. It allows for sleep, play, and time together with family or friends outside of work. This work setup also allows time for hobbies, exercise, or community involvement outside of the office. In short, team members can be well-rounded people, who are valuable to us as innovators and creators.

Long days are uncommon. Usually our office is dark and locked by six p.m. We work at the pace we do, with ample allotments for vacation, to help our team avoid burnout. If for some reason one day goes long, people can choose to take off earlier on another day and not cut into their vacation time. Our team members balance all of this themselves without having to ask permission; they use their accurate weekly time sheets to square up the worked hours.

Everyone starts off with four weeks of vacation time per year. While I'm sure there are Menlonians who have banked a lot of vacation time without using it—it doesn't expire—there are no institutional barriers to using your vacation, as we have no singular dependence on any team member.

In my previous jobs, I found that making your staff ask permission for time off creates fear-based guilt, and employees use this option less than they would if they were managing it themselves. A former manager once coached me against using my vacation time for family trips by trying to assure me that vacations weren't going to be as pleasant as I imagined. He, like most of my managers in my early career, made it clear that taking long vacations was a career-limiting move. I'm glad I never listened to that advice—our family vacations were some of the most wonderful memories I have.

If a team member is tired from being on the same project for too many weeks in a row, he or she can simply request a switch to a new project. We can usually accommodate that switch with little interruption. This makes for very little stress with any work assignment, as there is always an escape route if needed.

Finally, there is an unusual stress reliever at Menlo. Some call it attrition; we like to think of it as a sabbatical.

Honor People Over Process

James and I often shock our team members by reminding them we will help them find work elsewhere should they ever feel the desire to leave Menlo. We aren't trying to send them away. It's just that if someone at Menlo feels a yearning for a different experience for whatever reason, we want to encourage that person to pursue it. I believe this lowers unwanted attrition, but it also lends itself to the boomerangs who leave and come back later, energized, refreshed, and with a better understanding of what makes Menlo so special.

I believe most would surmise that a low attrition rate is a sign of a healthy culture. We make no such assertion. It's not that we want a high attrition rate—and we don't have one—but we don't see the value in being too careful about hiring and then hanging on to people you shouldn't or in trying to keep good people who, for one reason or another, want to move on or try something else. For all of these reasons, we don't pay attention to attrition. Anyway, it would be a complicated measurement, given the number of people who have left and come back to work at Menlo.

Legendary Michigan football coach Bo Schembechler once said that the hardest part of college football is graduating your top leaders every year, and the best part of college football is graduating your top leaders every year. We have many people on our team who have been with us for most of our history, and we would be very sad if they chose to leave us. But we would be the first to support them in their search if they thought it was time to pursue other endeavors.

Some of the worst cultures I have come to know are those from which no one ever leaves. Low attrition is not a sign of a healthy culture. Remember, not many people left East Berlin before the Iron Curtain fell. When it was time, they were *all* ready to leave—with sledgehammers. Ironically, in low-attrition cultures, the highest-paid people are likely the ones who tried to leave and were walled in with a counteroffer they couldn't refuse. They are still trapped. Higher pay doesn't erase that feeling.

Quality advocate Kristi S. recently told me she wants to leave Menlo and spend her summer working on a hops farm in western Michigan. She may be gone just for the summer, or maybe forever; we don't know how she will feel after she leaves or whether she will miss us and the work. If this is part of Kristi's dream and we try to get her to stay, what do we end up keeping? A team member with an unfulfilled dream, always wondering what could have been.

We think there's another option. Maybe Kristi leaves for a while, has a great time, and then decides to come back to Menlo. Perhaps she will have learned something new that she wouldn't have learned here, or she'll encounter great personal growth. In the best case, she wants to come back to Menlo, refreshed and ready to grow again here.

This stands in stark contrast to every managerial instinct I used to have. You might feel the same way. But keeping our relationships flexible keeps us strong.

High-Tech Anthropologist Carissa D. came to me one day and let me know she was leaving for a larger company, as she felt it was important to have that kind of experience on her résumé. Within four months at her new employer, she realized she enjoyed the environment at Menlo much more. She turned in her resignation notice, and her employer walked her out the door with security guards (a commonly reported practice). We had her back on the schedule at Menlo a day after she left her other employer.

Out of Office

In my experience, there's no replacement for a live, in-person company, with all members working in the same physical location. Being in the same space, with the sounds of your peers all around, greatly increases the possibility of innovation and collaboration. No advanced video conferencing system has gotten to the point where it's on par with being in the same physical location as the rest of your team.

For the same reasons that we try to avoid telecommuting, we are a one-location, single-room company. But if you have an offshore team, you may be curious how remote work arrangements would fit into a culture like ours. It's a natural question, given our global economy.

We actually ran a successful experiment in expanding the Menlo family with two of our former international interns. Michael and Femi, recent college graduates from Denmark and Northern Ireland, had become close friends during their year at Menlo. They also learned quite a bit from us about running an untraditional business. When it was time to return home to Europe, they decided to form a software consulting company called Arb Design, in honor of their time in Ann Arbor and at Menlo. I agreed to be their mentor—and their first client.

This offshore experiment worked very well because Michael and Femi were very well socialized with our team. As their first client, Menlo engaged Michael and Femi just as we did while they worked for us in Ann Arbor. They paired not with each other, but with Menlo programmers, using screen sharing technology, microphones, and speakers. They knew our practices and our culture from the year they'd spent with us. Having a great human relationship between the team members and a time zone difference that actually works for both sides are important factors.

I know some people have been able to sustain a marriage across distance or time, but it's not easy. Absence likely does make the heart grow fonder, but there is a limit beyond which you begin to forget important subtleties about the other person. I believe we have fooled ourselves as a society into thinking that remote work arrangements are actually more productive and effective, even though we are naturally wired as humans to be in community with one another. There is no better way to be in community than to actually spend time together in the same space.

I know this thinking will be controversial to many, and there are plenty of effective counterexamples. I'm just not going to spend any part of my remaining days trying to figure out how to make distance working part of our practice.

Although we do not, in general, allow telecommuting, we do make rare exceptions in the service of preserving our people. If someone at Menlo needs to work from home to care for a sick child or because there's a severe snowstorm on the way, we always work with our employees, though not as you might expect. We have experimented with different tactics to allow our team members to deal with their real lives and still participate in our daily work. One experiment consisted of using FaceTime on two iPads so that the team members working together could see and hear each other when one was unexpectedly called out of the office. When it was time for our daily standup, the iPad was brought to the meeting.

Kealy O., a longtime Menlo employee and one of our senior software developers, had a family situation that required her to be absent from the office and close to her parents. Her physical presence was required outside of the office, but she was otherwise available for work. In her words:

> **Last year my dad was diagnosed with cancer, and my mom** with severe anxiety issues. There were days and weeks missed from work. Thankfully, Menlo has the philosophy that family comes first. Missed days were never questioned.
>
> I explained my situation to the team and asked how they felt about remote pairing. Many were interested. I coordinated with the project manager to figure out what days of the week would work best. I spoke with James, explained the issue and our remote pairing idea, and said I didn't expect it to be permanent. I was hoping it would last only for one or two months. James expressed that he didn't want this to be the cultural norm but for a family crisis he was more than happy to support the experiment. The next week it was on the schedule.
>
> We used FaceTime to allow me to work in my programmer pair for a few weeks. This not only allowed me to hear my partner, but I could hear things going on at the office. And when I returned, other team members said they enjoyed hearing me, too. I appreciated even more that team members would still come and ask me questions. Likewise, if I had a question, my partner would just pick up the iPad and put it in front of others to have a conversation.

I'm so proud of our team when they care enough about each other to come up with temporary solutions for life emergencies or other personal needs. Yes, our process is important, but choosing process over people is not one of our core values.

A Ready State for Starting

Hiding inside all of this sustainability is another fundamental principle that Peter Drucker emphasized in his book *Management*. Management needs a *flexible* workforce. You can't have sustainability without flexibility. Flexibility gives you the best possible chance to start something new and innovative without killing the organization or the people inside of it.

How does a business practice being flexible? Is that even systematically possible? Drucker would likely have supported the notion that a company doesn't really grow until it is able to repetitively do the same thing again and again at a profit. Most companies differentiate by specializing, which means, over time, practicing less flexibility, not more. Kent Beck, among others, however, suggests we should embrace change.

In *Extreme Programming Explained*, Beck doesn't say, "Get along with change" or "Learn to live with change" or "Tolerate change." He says, "Embrace change." We embrace things we love. So we need to learn to love change, be open to flexibility, and understand the difference between flexibility that breeds chaos and flexibility that promotes sustainability.

A chaotic environment is very flexible, but not sustainable. At the opposite end, bureaucracy is the flexibility killer. That's why at Menlo we seek a simple structure: it gives us a place to start even in the face of great ambiguity.

Our simple structure is like chess. The board, the number and type of pieces, and the rules for movement are easy to understand. But chess is also an extremely complex game, even with this very simple structure. There are billions upon billions of variations possible once you reach the middle game, yet chess masters apply a limited set of well-studied opening moves to get the match under way.

Most companies are very unpracticed at starting new initiatives. Starting a new initiative is so difficult that this inability to *begin* often leaves even the best of ideas stalled. If the initiative does kick off and gets off to a bad start, each day that goes by makes it more difficult to get back on track. This is a key reason most companies are frozen in place and can't figure out how to try anything new: they don't know how to *begin*.

We're more like chess players. In our story card system, we have decks of starter cards that are likely to occur in any new project. They won't all be useful for a given project, and they won't all be sufficient either, but these starter cards give us a quick and simple flexible start to any new project, regardless of domain or technology.

Vision Is Key

Zingerman's Deli started in a thirteen-hundred-square-foot Ann Arbor storefront in 1982. By 1992, founders Paul Saginaw and Ari Weinzweig could feel the itch of entrepreneurial ambition. Should they franchise the deli? No, they wanted Zingerman's to be unique. Thus began a two-year visioning process that allowed them to picture and pursue a new beginning: a community of businesses in Ann Arbor focused on delivering flavorful traditional food with a staff dedicated to offering a great Zingerman's experience.

Zingerman's is now an empire worth $40 million–plus per year, with a community of nine different businesses (so far) that all deliver the brand consistently, despite each one being unique. These include the original but now much expanded deli, a coffee company, a bakehouse, a creamery, a sit-down restaurant, a training company, and a mail-order company, among others.

One of the biggest lessons Zingerman's learned during this process is how to start any new initiative, no matter how big or small.

It starts with a vision. No vision, no new project. End of story. Their very specific formula for vision is described in *A Lapsed Anarchist's Approach to Building a Great Business*, the first of Ari's book series. Their ZingTrain company also teaches the visioning process in a wonderful course.

Having a repeatable, simple, and compelling way to start a new initiative is key to avoid being stuck in the starting blocks. Usually, once anything is off to a great start, momentum is created and sustains the new initiative even through difficult periods.

Flexibility

Even if you know how to start new projects and initiatives, your team must also constantly stretch and practice organizational flexibility. Otherwise, we might be able to start a new initiative, but there won't be anybody to help carry it forward beyond the most passionate visionaries.

At Menlo, flexibility is ingrained in every facet of our system. You see it everywhere.

SPACE: Inflexible work space can defeat new initiatives because new endeavors might have needs different from anything you've done before. Keep your space flexible. Don't put the bureaucracy of facilities departments or "permission asking" between your team and the space they operate in. As you've already learned, our team sometimes changes the space just for fun. Let your team do the same.

INDIVIDUALS: Our pairs are assigned and they switch every week. Every week each team member must flexibly adjust to the personality and work style of another Menlonian. We all believe in the same system, but we are all very different. Having to adjust to these differences every week produces a flexible mind-set in every team member. The weekly switching may also include changing projects, domains, or technologies. Part of being flexible means staying in learning mode. Practicing how to learn keeps us a learning organization, which contributes to the team's continuous mental adaptability.

COGNITIVE DIVERSITY: We don't offer referral bonuses, so we don't get a bunch of folks from the same organization, which would diminish team flexibility. Because we don't just focus our recruiting efforts on local universities and talent pools, we gain a cognitive diversity of people who have been taught in different ways by different professors. People from all age ranges, with varied life experiences, also work together to keep us flexible.

WORKWEEK: Our flexibility on individual schedules and the continuity that pairing offers mean we can also accommodate part-time workers. This level of flexibility again opens up a part of the workforce that isn't usually available to all companies. This might mean there is a student who can work only three days a week during the school year. A full-time team member is paired with another Menlonian on the days the part-timer isn't there.

Scheduling is definitely tricky and is one of the most thoughtful processes we go through every week. But this scheduling process is also at the center of our organizational flexibility.

DOMAINS: As a software company, we're often asked what technologies we specialize in. The truth is, none of them, or, alternatively, all of them. By practicing with all of the various technologies, we achieve a team flexibility and openness to learning that allow us to flex into new technical regions without fear. We also don't pigeonhole team members into subtechnical domains such as database, front end, etc. Nor do we "make work" just to keep subtechnical domain experts busy while we are waiting for their expertise to be needed again.

ROLES: Because people, not skills, are our most important resource, we do everything to keep our best people, even if it means moving them into different roles. On occasion, people on our team decide to try other roles: programmers become High-Tech Anthropologists, project managers do QA, and just about every other kind of switch you can imagine. We resisted this at the beginning as we were trying to establish clear definitions of each role, but now we've reached the point where it is a much easier experiment to run with any team member interested. If a team member tries a new role and it doesn't work out, he or she can always go back. This helps with the anxiety of change and adds to a flexible mind-set.

This attitude toward roles gives us a more flexible team. At any given moment of project stage and mix, we may need more High-Tech Anthropologists and fewer programmers, or vice versa. Our pairing approach ensures that experienced role models are available as pair partners to help those who are switching roles to come up to speed quickly.

TOOLS: Since most of our tools are simple, cheap, and usually paper based, anyone can run a cheap "tool" experiment without asking permission.

An important part of our High-Tech Anthropology practice is simple prototyping. Most of the prototypes are paper based, but can include tools as varied as duct tape and old yogurt containers cut to fit a design idea. This simple, cheap, fast (and fun) prototyping technique infects the rest of the organization, and we try simple new stuff all the time.

In contrast, if some crazy new idea first required a large capital outlay just to run an experiment, we would all be nervous and cautious. Fear would stymie the experiment.

COMPUTERS: Most teams like ours want to standardize their computer equipment. At Menlo we make sure to diversify our equipment. This means some parts of our system are more expensive to support. Standardization would ensure simpler maintenance, much the same way Southwest Airlines enjoys lower overall costs by standardizing on Boeing 737s. However, this would put us at risk for creating software that works really well on one type of computer, or screen size, or processor speed, or memory configuration, or operating system but then works poorly or not at all on other computers or software configurations.

Each week, as the pairs switch, they will likely have to switch computers, too. This guarantees that no one can blame a faulty program on "it worked on my machine." If we are to build software that is user friendly, we need to keep ourselves flexible on what equipment we use as well.

Flexibility Produces Capacity That Is Ready When You Need It

If you aren't systematically adding capacity to your team, then when new unexpected business needs arise, overtime is the only option for additional capacity. Hiring is usually not an option because there is no capacity to quickly onboard new people in most organizations. The required overtime will typically be lopsided; one part of the organization will be working overtime and another part will have little to do. This breeds a feeling of unfairness. The underworked feel guilty for leaving work on time while their overworked peers are staying late and getting stressed. There is little comfort in the guilty thinking that their day will come.

During this stressful time, quality begins to diminish and customer service suffers. Organizational demoralization starts to creep in, and everyone begins to believe, *This is just the way things are around here.* We have almost all experienced the customer side of this equation at a restaurant when, by some strange formula of restaurant table allocations, our server is completely overworked while others are standing around chatting with one another.

One of our longtime customers recently called and asked if some team members could attend a major planning session for their future product directions. The call came in on a Thursday afternoon—and the weeklong meeting was starting on Monday morning. The folks we would typically send to such a meeting were scheduled for other assignments or were due to go on vacation. Two team members, Tracy and Carol, raised their hands and volunteered to go. Since they had been in planning games with this client, had taken part in Show & Tells, and knew the company well, they were ready to go with only one day's notice. They performed flawlessly; our customer later thanked me for sending an "A" team on such short notice.

Too often, businesses go to the same people every time to do the same work, all the while never building capacity for unexpected needs. In our world, pairing is a central element in building this capacity. Each team member's immersion in our belief system and the willingness of the leaders to trust people to step out of their typical day-to-day role and into a new role create a different kind of joy that emanates from the trust shown both in the people and the system.

We constantly look for ways to build capacity so that we have the flexibility necessary to respond when change occurs, as it always will. The flexible nature of our team, coupled with their willingness to embrace change, gives us something most teams can't even begin to imagine: simple scalability.

Scalability

Adding manpower to a late software project makes it later.

—BROOKS'S LAW

FRED BROOKS, *The Mythical Man-Month*

I'm pleased to report that Brooks's Law can be broken.

Brooks's Law is the motto of a broken hero-based culture that still largely exists in software development today. It states that the onboarding cost of a new person, particularly to a late project, far exceeds the potential contribution of that new person within the first few weeks or months of joining an effort. If a project is already late, then adding someone to it will make it later. The only alternative to a missed deadline then is an eighty-hour-per-week death march for the current team.

While Brooks's attention was focused predominantly on software teams, this principle applies to any discipline or organization that has no structured approach to adding new people. If you have no systematic means of transferring knowledge in a way that can quickly lead to mastery and autonomy for the new person, Brooks's Law applies to you, too.

Many industries are faced with similar "truths" like Brooks's Law that everyone assumes are unassailable and absolute facts, rather than traditions waiting for change. The Vienna General Hospital of the 1800s likely assumed high maternal death rates were an unassailable and unavoidable truth. Orville Wright thought that the biggest airplane that could ever be built would carry only two passengers. As with any theorem, all that is required is *one* counterexample to disprove it.

Scalability is a very important topic in business circles. Investors and business plan competition judges will always ask if your idea or your business is scalable. If not, your idea is not interesting to them. If a business can't scale, it is probably an indication of faulty "systems." Brooks's Law states it emphatically: you can't expect to scale software teams once the project is under way. Brooks appropriately indicted an entire industry that uses improperly organized systems. Software teams couldn't scale because they were (and often still are) built on a hero-based model, and heroes are hard to scale. Heroes won't have the time to train up another hero—they are too busy—so scaling up is impossible. And if you scale down, you lose heroes and there is no one to replace them.

At Menlo, we have defeated Brooks's Law so many times that its premise is but a faint reminder of a quaint time in our industry's history. Our entire process is focused on breaking this law. Pairing, switching the pairs, automated unit testing, code stewardship, non-hero-based hiring, constant conversation, open work environment, and visible artifacts all topple Brooks's assertion with ease. As you will read below, our system also trivializes an aspect of scaling that no one ever considers: scaling down.

Every business faces the question of scalability in wishing to improve business results. Walmart looked to information technology to solve discount retail scalability. McDonald's turned to consistency in ingredients, menu, and staff process. Zingerman's chose visioning to scale from one business to a dozen and beyond. Southwest Airlines found scalability by standardizing on a single aircraft, the Boeing 737.

As you consider your own organization, ask yourself:

- Do you have trouble finding the right talent to match your needs?
- Are you regularly disappointed with new staff after just a few months?

- Do you have the flexibility to shift underused talent into the high-need areas?
- Do you resist new opportunities because you can't find the talent you need?
- Do you keep adding new business without increasing the staff?
- If a project is slowing down, do you just keep the project team busy?
- Do you lie awake trying to think through better answers to these questions?

Practice Scaling

Our pairing system, particularly the part where we switch the pairs every week, gives us a chance to practice scalability even when we don't need it. We borrowed this concept from the airline industry (there it is called cockpit resource management). By switching pairs every week, we practice onboarding a new team member into a project even if the project stays the same size. We also practice onboarding new team members by bringing in four to six international interns annually.

If we have four programmers—two pairs—working on the same project, we switch these pairs every week. Just with these same four programmers we have three weeks' worth of combinations before they begin to duplicate rotations. After a few weeks, we will bring in another programmer and send one of the original four off to another project.

You may wonder how this is actually *practicing* to be scalable if the team members joining are actually doing work. This is perhaps the most beautiful part of all. The work *is* the means of practicing.

As new team members join a project's effort, the existing team members have to practice how to bring them up to speed, while getting the work of the card done. Meanwhile, if the team stays the same size, someone has to roll off, and some amount of knowledge and expertise is lost. In this transition, the team adjusts to that change and practices for scaling down.

This basic style of pairing and repairing, of onboarding and offboarding, continues to strengthen the team's preparation for a moment of scaling.

True Scalability Works in Both Directions

Most business gurus consider scalability only in the growth direction. When someone asks the question "Can this scale?" he or she is thinking only about scaling up. We believe an appropriately designed system can scale in both directions with the same alacrity.

Scale Up

Say a client comes in to Menlo and asks that we double the speed on a project that has four programmers working on it. In our world, this translates directly into twice as many hours of effort required on story cards laid out on twice as many of our planning sheets. Our project managers work with our Factory Floor Manager during the resource planning, and they ask for four more programmers for the next week of this project. The original four will likely be assigned to this project in the next week's resource plan to scale up efforts. We would then add in any others who have also done rotations to that point in the project's history. The team is rounded out with others available to rotate in. Voilà! The next week, twice as many cards are assigned and nearly twice as much work is getting done.

The space helps with the scaling, as the team will pull over two tables and two computers into its pod of tables for this project and, with no fuss at all, the expanded team is colocated. High-Speed Voice Technology can then be used to further enhance knowledge transfer. As the basic planning and coding practices are consistent across all projects, there is no need to train these new team members in any project-localized or personality-based methodology. The fact that everyone on the team has a shared belief system in our approach ensures there is no friction around these shifts in project assignment.

This is such a common occurrence in Menlo's world, no one in the sequence, including our client, would even question the validity of such a scaling-up request.

Scale Down

There are times when projects must shrink as well. If the client needs to reduce budgetary burn rate, or the project has simply reached a point where less work is required, scaling down follows the same sequence. Because the team is not based on towers of knowledge, because no one developer owns part of the code, because everyone has been working in all sections of the code, and because the people who have moved to another project are still in the same room and within eyeshot and earshot of one another, there is no meaningful loss of information about the project.

How does a team get back up to speed when the project has been placed on the back burner for months at a time? Can scaling down work when the project scales to zero? Is it possible to restart a project after months on hold, or go back in to add new features to a completed project? This falls back to documentation and standard work process. The automated unit tests provide the first foundation. They catch misunderstandings as new coding changes happen. If a programming pair returns to the project, makes a change they believe is okay, and one or more of the unit tests fail, the automated tests inform the programmers immediately that a mistake was made. This begins to refresh their memory of decisions made in the past. Code stewardship is also a big part of this, as the code has been viewed and adapted by so many different people over time that it has evolved into a body of work that reflects a commonly understood expression of intent, not a convoluted expression understood only by the hero originator and no one else.

[199]

What you are seeing beginning to develop in the software industry is a set of standards like those that evolved in the building industry. When a renovation crew walks into a fairly modern home, they can be sure that there are two-by-four studs every sixteen inches and that an electrical circuit and its associated circuit breaker (an example of an automated unit test) will ensure that the correct current level will flow down a wire that would otherwise melt and burn if this limit was exceeded.

Build in Slack to Handle Scaling

This would work so beautifully if, across all of our active projects, the need to scale up and scale down perfectly balanced out and meshed exactly with vacation schedules. Maybe somewhere things would work that way, but here on Planet Menlo, it's never smooth and perfect. To give ourselves slack in case we need to add or drop members to a client project, we've built buffering elements in to our system. These are internal projects that can receive extra team members or be cannibalized as required, or clever business arrangements with willing clients who let us scale their projects up or down by a small percentage in exchange for discounted services. Some of our longest-term and most trusting clients also allow us to move team members in and out of their projects when it makes business sense to do so.

It's not difficult for us to add more team members if our capacity needs to stretch beyond the existing Menlo team. We have a very healthy community of independent subcontractors who help us out when we need it. If we need to add to our overall capacity, we can schedule an Extreme Interview and hire new full-timers. We always have a pile of applicants ready to be called in when we are ready, having built up an interested base of potential staff through our tours, classes, and general community outreach.

Lean manufacturing principles teach industrial operations engineers to build slack into their systems in order to operate at peak efficiency. Funny—this would suggest that we have learned to treat our machines better than we have learned to treat our humans. So many businesses operate at or near 100 percent utilization and, with overtime, sometimes well beyond 100 percent. Symptoms of this mania include working vacations, the stoppage of projects when only one person takes time off, and constant overtime and overwhelming work from home. I refuse to accept that as a proper way to treat people.

Brooks's Law still applies in the rest of our industry. If a scaling-up request is made of a traditionally organized team, the only alternative is to ask for overtime. Suddenly programmers aren't working forty to fifty hours per week, but eighty to one hundred hours. This can last about a week before very tired human programmers start introducing more quality problems than new functionality. At this point, the project's gravestone is being carved at the local stonecutter and the plot is being dug out back. There will be a memorial service soon, lamenting the loss of another project. This happens to the tune of about $75 billion *per year* in our industry, according to the annual CHAOS Report issued by the Standish Group.

If we need to get more done, we add more people. It's that simple.

Although I'm confident we can scale up to at least 150 people with our current structure, I know we would have to continue to embrace changes in our practices to adjust to larger staff size and project workload. Check back with me in a decade. As we've grown, we've continued to maintain, enhance, and extend our culture to reach new levels of staff size and project workload. As of 2013, we have tripled our space three times since our inception. Our team size has increased tenfold. For us, that is good enough proof that we can scale up. In the decade between 2001 and 2011, there were a few global calamities, wars, and economic downturns that required us to prove we could also scale down.

I am pretty sure our current system would not work for a thousand people on the same project, as if that is common. Many conclude that if it can't work at a thousand people, it isn't really a scalable system. It's not that it's impossible; it's that we just don't know what we would look like at a thousand people or what we'd have to change to accomplish this. It doesn't invalidate our ability to scale.

When Henry Ford built the Willow Run plant to manufacture B24 bombers during World War II, the initial production rate was about one a day in 1941. By 1944, when pressed, his team improved the systems and processes in the same plant and began producing one an hour. Scaling a process-based organization is a thoughtful pursuit; scaling a hero-based environment is insanity.

Link Scalability with Sustainability

> If you scale and destroy quality in the process, have you
>   really scaled?
> If you scale and destroy your team's morale, spirit, and
>   energy, have you really scaled?

> If you scale and threaten people's lives in the process, have
> you really scaled?
> If you scale and are defeated in the marketplace by
> superior products, have you really scaled?
> If you can scale up but can't scale down, can you really
> say you are able to scale at all?

Our definition of joy means that we must be able to scale and still produce quality products and maintain our culture.

Measuring Joy

Most people who visit think all of this is pretty neat—until they consider the effect on cost. They quickly surmise that scaling the way we do must make software development at least twice as expensive.

How exactly would they like to measure cost? If we are measuring cost at the speed of typing in lines of code, then yes, I suppose, we are twice as expensive. If any of us in our industry really believed that typing was the primary cost of development, every computer science curriculum in the nation would make a typing class a prerequisite for a degree. They might even make a typing speed test part of their admissions requirements.

At Menlo, we measure cost against the final product: *joy*. We want the end users of our work product to thank us someday and tell us they love what we created for them. Most software teams never even get *close* to this effect. Can you measure something as intangible as joy? Perhaps not exactly, but you can measure usage, long-term quality, market share, customer satisfaction, market dominance, end user delight (at least anecdotally), and a lack of support calls. If we establish the team's accountability to get these kinds of results every time, we get to joy.

THIRTEEN

Accountability and Results

There are two freedoms—the false, where a man is free to do what he likes; the true, where he is free to do what he ought.

—CHARLES KINGSLEY

S everal years ago, I was in Atlanta teaching Menlo's practices to a company that does car sales online and in print. I had their entire technical team and management team in the room, all day. In the middle of the session, I started speaking about our version of accountability. At Menlo, we believe that in order for accountability to produce the desired results, it must be circular. There must be accountability all around the table.

As CEO, I shouldn't expect any greater commitment from my team than I am willing to offer in return. This simple formula builds trust—the kind of trust that leads to commitment without fear. In my description, I thoroughly described how all this works by using our estimating practice as an example. My commitment to the team is that I will teach and reinforce the estimation system I am about to describe, and I will ensure that our customers adhere to this system.

As you've learned, we have a weekly estimation session. The pairs estimate the active story cards. Our first commitment to the team is that they will never be intimidated or cajoled about their estimates. Each pair's estimates are sacred to that pair. While there can be healthy discussion, a project manager cannot override a pair's estimate. At this point, I was already starting to sense discomfort in the room. The facial expressions and rolling eyes told me that I was starting to hit nerves.

I went on to describe that when the work is actually assigned, the pair always gets the amount of time they estimated without equivocation. If a pair says a card will take sixteen hours, they will get two days to work on it. The room grew quieter.

Finally, I added that if the pair goes over their estimate, there would be no consequences, no punishment, and no demerits. The client will be billed for the extra hours and expected to pay for the work. You could have heard a pin drop at this point.

We trust our team, I said, and believe they do the best job they can during estimation and while doing the work. But sometimes things go wrong and end up being more difficult than we expect. We will learn from this estimating mistake, and we will do better next time. In this trusted system of estimating, I can ask the team to share bad news as soon as they know it.

If a pair has worked two hours on a sixteen-hour card and they discovered a problem that will cause them to exceed the estimated hours, I simply ask that they share that information with their project manager. We have taught our project managers to thank the team with a smile for sharing what they've learned. If the impact is going to affect the total results we expect to deliver to the customer that week, the project manager must then share this bad news with the client and ask them how they'd like us to handle it. Would they like us to just keeping going and potentially threaten completion of a lower-priority card? Or would they like us to stop work on the card whose estimate has just ballooned?

The covenant between client and Menlo is such that the story card and its estimate are the atomic elements of our process. When those two come together, we then have a basis for defining work and getting to results. You don't get the estimate you want; you get the estimate you need to produce a quality software product. The estimate has integrity. The estimate is honest. The people who do the work create the estimate, and we trust them. However, it is just an estimate, a *best guess* based on the information we had at the time.

At this point, the silence in the room where I was lecturing was deafening. I clearly had struck a dissonant chord within their culture. I paused, waiting for the inevitable questions that result from this seemingly paradoxical explanation of accountability. I got more than I'd bargained for when Joe, a VP of marketing, stood up and pointed an accusatory index finger at me.

"This is bullshit!" he said sternly and with great conviction.

At their company, they had real accountability, he said. If you estimated that something would be done by Friday and it wasn't done, you were going to stay the weekend and meet your commitment. It didn't matter whether it was your kid's birthday this weekend; you'd catch the birthday next year. The work needed to be completed. "That's accountability," he told me and everyone else in the room.

The room remained silent as he stood and stared me down. I'm sure everyone was wondering how I was going to handle this little exchange. He was fired up. I was pretty calm.

I asked Joe what he thought might happen if Menlo switched to his version of accountability. He reflected for a few seconds. Then I could literally see his mind changing, his emotions shift, cell by cell from head to toe. He responded in a very different tone.

"They'd start to pad their estimates," he said. "The project managers would catch this and start trimming estimates based on this padding. The team would start lying about actually being done, and then quality would start to go down the drain. Suddenly, we'd have all kinds of support problems and a demoralized team where no one trusted anyone. You'd have at Menlo *exactly* what we have here at our company."

Joe learned an important lesson that day, one rooted in human nature. Humans have a good instinct for fairness and will rebel, often silently, when their fairness meter detects unethical imbalance. Without trust and commitment all around the accountability table, accountability doesn't produce results.

In our world, the CEO commits to a system and stands by it in good times and bad. The project managers further understand that their role is not fearmonger. The team understands that honesty is rewarded. Our clients understand they have a role to play as well.

This system produces the results everyone is seeking. Having removed fear from estimation, the team estimates more aggressively. Knowing they are working toward a goal they set for themselves, a pair of workers will push to hit their own estimate. The client will actually get more work done in less time, as long as they are willing to acknowledge that, sometimes, an estimate will be wrong. Add to this that quality will not be compromised, and you now have the results most teams can only dream about.

Predictable Structures Hold Everyone Accountable

Jen Baird, a client CEO, was in for a visit, and just for fun I suggested we test our structure for weakness. We walked up to a pair of Menlo programmers and suggested a change to the system they were working on, a system Jen's company was paying us to build. The pair instantly responded by grabbing a story card and prepared to write down Jen's new request. We told the pair we didn't have time for that—but they ignored us and started writing down the request anyway. When they were done, they instructed Jen and me to take the story card over to Lisa, the project manager for Jen's project. Lisa would assign the next number and work with the team to estimate the story card and figure out where it could fit into that week's plan.

Jen and I tried to interrupt the system, but we couldn't. Even the CEO and the client couldn't budge the accountability measure set in place. Ours is the only system we've found that enforces and supports accountability without fear, ambiguity, or intimidation. Most accountability breaks down when existing systems are ignored or worked around to get the *real* work done.

Our strongest mechanism for accountability is our story card–driven "five-day iterative cycle," executed every week without fail since June 12, 2001. *All* client work is done within this cycle. *No* exception. *Ever.* Tens of thousands of hours of work per year, every single year, good economy years and bad, since 2001. The five-day cycle follows a predictable pattern, and that pattern is known and expected by everyone on the team, including our clients.

If a structured process is easy to understand and use, there is no reason *not* to use it. No one at Menlo (including me) can ever say, "Well, this task that just came up is really important and we don't have time to use our process." It would actually take us more time to not use our process. At Menlo, we are *all* held accountable to our process. We believe in that process. We know it produces quality results.

Accountability Through Choices

In our early days, we worked on a big East Coast pharmaceutical software project. The client used a traditional budgeting system, where the money allocated for a project needed to be spent by a certain date. In this case, three hundred thousand dollars had to be spent by December 31. Not one penny more or less, and not a day late. Our project manager had laid out the plan for the entire project. In preparation for the plan review teleconference with the client, she asked me to review some things prior to the call.

My review of the plan took place about five minutes before the scheduled call. I took one look and declared it was a bad plan. All the blood drained from the project manager's face as she wondered what flaws I could see so quickly. The obvious problem was that her project planning included feature development right up to the last minute of the last day of the project. In any project, feature development nearly always introduces some bugs, and we need to build capacity in our schedule to deal with troubleshooting our work.

How many bugs did she think we'd have to fix before the project was complete? I asked. As we hadn't even started the project yet, she explained she didn't know that yet. I asked her to guess how many. Under duress (as the call was quickly approaching), she blurted, "Six." I grabbed six cards and wrote "Bug 1" through "Bug 6" on them. We speedily worked together to estimate these potential bugs, allocating from two hours to thirty-two hours of work on each of these imagined problems. Before I walked away, I asked her to put them in the plan.

When I caught up with her after the call, she relayed that her call had gone very well. The client was amazed at her foresight in building bug fixing into the estimate; they had never seen a vendor predict problems before they existed. They were quite impressed. This level of accountability felt like joy to me.

Our planning game sets us up so perfectly for accountability and empowerment. If a project's sponsor wants something in the plan, he or she picks up a folded story card and places it on the planning sheet. If the sponsor doesn't want it in the plan, it is left on the table. There is no need for high emotion during planning times, no need to scream about how this or that thing should be in the plan. If you want it in the plan, put it on the planning sheet. If you've run over the established budget, then you must take something off to make room. This removes the fear-based negotiation that often occurs during a more traditional planning effort. No one can say, "C'mon, guys, just fit this one extra little thing in, okay?" Everyone knows that, *sure*, we can fit in one more thing, as long as we remove something else. Planning becomes a conversation rather than an innuendo-based power play.

If there is concern about unknowns or estimates that don't pan out, then we simply take a percentage of planning sheets and write the word *Contingency* on them as placeholders for the normal, healthy fear of the unknown. In this way, we have two parties acknowledging there are some things we don't know, and the unknown is made obvious.

Showcasing Your Work Is Accountability in Action

The greatest benefit of our weekly Show & Tell is that it allows us to walk through each completed story card with our client, itself a performance of accountability. Show & Tell creates a powerful feedback loop between the conceptual process of planning and the practical output of our work. Better yet, we again demonstrate circular accountability by having our client show us the work we did the previous week. We are making ourselves vulnerable by not controlling where the client goes with the software, and the client is demonstrating great interest by investing the time to touch the work we've done.

If we didn't get everything done that was planned, it will be obvious in the Show & Tell. Sometimes we don't get everything done owing to resource constraints on our side. Other times we don't get something done because we're stuck awaiting additional information from our client. In this case, we indicate the card's status with a red dot and a Post-it note, explaining what and perhaps whom we are waiting on to answer a question. This leads to another interesting aspect of circular accountability: it reveals any difference between stated priority and actual priority. If our client thought a certain card was important enough to schedule this week but didn't have time to answer our question, it's very evident why the card

wasn't completed. While valuing transparency, this is a very democratic way to hold your client accountable.

Actual Actuals

In 2009, I presented to about four hundred attendees at a Project
Management Institute Global Congress in Orlando, Florida. PMI
is the certifying body for all project management professionals.

I decided to run an experiment. I asked the audience to raise
their hands if the Project Management Institute certified them as
Project Management Professionals. Four hundred hands went into
the air. I asked them to raise their hands again if they had signed an
oath of ethical standards to receive their certification. Again, all
four hundred raised their hand.

Next, I instructed them to close their eyes. Project managers are
very good at following rules, particularly from authority figures, so
they all behaved. I then asked them to raise their hands if they had
ever been forced to fake actuals for a project they managed, in viola-
tion of their signed personal oath. All four hundred hands were
slowly raised. Wow. Clearly, fear manufactured by authority figures
produces unethical behavior even in the most honest people.

I have a profound respect for the Project Management Institute
and project managers in general. The real trouble is not with this
organization, its goals, or its teachings, nor with the professionals it
certifies. The manufactured fear of management they operate under
is enough to wilt any capable individual, no matter how professional, knowledgeable, or experienced.

The real problem, as I see it, is not only that all of these professionals reported fake actuals but that the fake data was later treated
as accurate and factual and used to plan future efforts. This is one
of the main reasons that project budgets are always inadequate,

which causes problems along the way and eventually cancellations due to cost overruns.

One of the greatest benefits of an accountability that doesn't rely on fear is that we get *actual* actuals. "Actuals" refers to the amount of time something *actually* takes versus how much time it's estimated to take.

We keep very detailed time sheets at Menlo. All time spent on a client project is logged in on a weekly time sheet, and team members record their time against each story card that is worked on. Accurate time sheets are turned in to the Factory Floor Manager by Monday morning at eight a.m. every week. All time is then assembled into a project-tracking spreadsheet. We preview and review a weekly client invoice that reflects the time spent, which is then mailed to the client and archived. The cycle repeats every five days, fifty-two weeks a year. Our clients can never come to the end of a project and be surprised at the time spent on their work or with the billing.

The first benefit of accurate timekeeping is that each pair gets a chance to reflect on the accuracy of its original estimate and what may have led to a big underage or overage. The second benefit is that there is great value in the aggregate information we collect across all projects every week. Our entire company history of actual data gives us a key advantage in sizing future projects. We know with complete certainty, down to a quarter of an hour, exactly how many hours past projects required. When we explore potential projects, we can look through our historical data and find comparable projects to give us a reliable idea of how much effort this potential project will likely take.

Our accurate data often confounds our sales process, as we are typically compared to what appear to be lower-cost competitors. Our experience tells us again and again, however, that our competitors have no idea how long things take because they don't keep *actual* actuals themselves. We have had a number of clients choose the lower-cost competitor but then come back later amazed at how accurate our original estimate was. It's a painful and costly lesson for some. I had one CEO call me back after such a failure to tell me he would never choose the lowest-priced competitor again.

Most organizations are really bad at keeping track of how they spend their time. Some professionals consider it an affront to track their hours. My guess is that they wish to hide something. We worked with one organization that embedded one of their team members in our project team. We asked him to fill out a time sheet like every member of our team, which we needed to keep our actuals accurate. It turned out it might have been the first accurate time sheet he ever submitted in his life. As he later told us, the boss back at his own organization insisted his time sheets always report forty hours—never less, never more. Not only is this request unethical, but the company is refusing to acknowledge how much time is actually needed to complete any given project. Their time data is completely useless for future planning.

Get Results by Giving Your Team a Chance to Get Things *Done*

There are lots of books written about employee engagement with top ten lists that count the ways to keep employees engaged. Some mention having a great boss, others a short commute to work, and still others a fun work environment.

The one that resonates most with me for long-lasting team engagement is *the ability to go to work and get meaningful things done*. Not just started, talked about, or delegated, but actually *done*—finished, wrapped up, and delivered. It doesn't matter how simple or hard the task or even whether you had to work longer hours to get there. *Done* releases endorphins, the body's natural opiate, and it's addictive.

Done, when it really means done and behind you, leads to the joy of knowing that a hard day of work produced a valuable and valued accomplishment.

We have so many channels to interrupt us these days. Phone calls, e-mails, bosses stopping by to say, "How's it going?," meetings where new priorities are set without any consideration for yesterday's commitments, and unplanned emergencies all distract us from our plan for the day. We want to believe we thrive on multitasking.

Dealing with all of these competing and conflicting priorities usually occurs in an environment of total ambiguity. Most of us have a general idea where our company is headed and how our department fits into that direction, and a few specific ideas on what our own individual role is. But once Monday morning comes, the inevitable question that arises in the first deep breath is: "What exactly should I be working on today?"

When the boss does stop by and asks the inevitable "What are you working on?" you randomly pick one of your obvious competing priorities. You usually pick something difficult enough that he will leave you alone for most of the day with the confidence that he has properly managed you, and then after offering some bland "Go get 'em" inspiration, he shrugs and walks away. You realize he has no idea what you were supposed to be working on and the question was simply a matter of confirming that you were working on *something* related to the ambiguous goals and activities of the organization.

Your feeble defense against interruptions crumbles about fourteen minutes later when the phones ring, unplanned meetings are called, emergencies pull you away, and your day is now off to the races. Before you know it, the day is over without your actually having gotten anything *done*.

There is nothing more debilitating than coming into work and not knowing what you should be working on. Perhaps this is why I have so much disdain for job ads that declare "self-starter" in their description. A worker has a right to know what is expected of him or her, and the clearer that is, the more joy the employee will have when getting it done.

Our simple pushpin wallboard displays give that structure to everyone on our team. Because all team members know the process by which those cards ended up in their swim lane, they have the confidence to know they are working on something the client actually cares about. The greater freedom in our wallboard display, however, is that *everyone* can see what work is assigned to *everyone else*. The implicit fairness that humans crave is right there for everyone to see.

As the piece of yarn that is stretched across the work authorization board moves down day by day in a clocklike fashion, schedule performance is easy to discern. If there are yellow dots above the string, we know exactly where we are behind our original plan. If there are orange dots or green dots below the string, we know exactly where we are ahead of plan. To us, this is simply information— we don't view "behind plan" as problematic or "ahead of plan" as a victory. There is no fear for a pair of partners in having a yellow dot above the string. Their accountability is to make sure their project manager is aware of how long a delay is anticipated so that appropriate business decisions can be made. They are also accountable for doing good work that prevents quality problems and for making sure they haven't cut any corners.

If one pair is ahead and another is behind, the first pair will offer to help the other. Since the team works a sustainable forty-hour workweek pace, the partners aren't angling to stay off the critical path, put their feet up, and let another pair suffer. At Menlo, we've developed a team that believes in joint ownership of all the cards assigned. There is no delight in faulting one pair for not completing a card.

Sometimes we get *everything* done early. The client knows this happens occasionally and they choose "pull-ahead" story cards that are available for scheduling if the team runs out of work for that week. We had one big project where the team kept completing all of the cards assigned way ahead of schedule. They got so much done early that we also ran out of pull-ahead cards, and the project manager needed to ask the client to prioritize more work for the week.

While many traditional management teams would delight in this situation, our team actually found it all quite annoying. Something had broken in our estimating efforts. Perhaps fear had somehow silently crept in and all pairs were estimating high. We talked about it, and within a few weeks everything was back on track.

Freedom's Rewards

Menlo's simple, unambiguous system of collecting new requirements on handwritten index cards, estimating time, planning, executing, and showing the results is repeated every week for every client project, no matter how big or small. There are no special cases in which the process is abandoned by edict or client personality. Our test of a good process is that when things get rough, people on the team run toward the process rather than away from it. Perhaps above all else, our team feels accountable to our process, as it provides the structure and freedom they crave. Our structure makes them feel safe and in control. Who wouldn't want to be accountable to a system like that?

The planning game process is well understood by our clients. They know we can bill them only for the work they've authorized in a planning game. If they don't plan with us, their project stops. It doesn't stop because we are pounding our feet and demanding adherence; it stops because it would make no sense for us to do work that isn't authorized by our client.

I am always amazed when people ask me where we find clients who are willing to spend two to four hours per week steering their multimillion-dollar mission-critical project. If the project is so important, the real question is, who *wouldn't* be willing to put in that time and activity? The difference in our structured process is that these few hours of client engagement each week pull the client into a very productive and unambiguous conversation about their mission-critical effort.

Real engagement for Menlonians works because our team *unambiguously knows* what is expected of them. The client cares enough to come in and plan their project by picking the cards they want us to work on. Our team knows that all the cards in their lane are cards the client has chosen, and that the client is coming in just a few days later to earnestly review their work in Show & Tell. Most important, the folks at Menlo know they have the freedom to do their work, unfettered by bureaucracy.

People who work in this environment also have another critical fulfilling and energizing element driving them: they get the chance to do the best job they can possibly do.

Trust, accountability, and results: these get you to joy.

FOURTEEN

Alignment

Make me one with everything.

—ZEN MASTER,
placing his order at Le Dog, a famous Ann Arbor hot dog stand

I always knew I would start a company someday. I never thought it would take me past my forty-third birthday to make that happen. To prepare myself along the way, I sought to learn more about how to run a business, since my computer science degrees and skills wouldn't be enough to sustain the kind of business I wanted. As my career progressed, I sought out smaller firms that afforded me the opportunity to wear many hats and gain valuable start-up experience while still getting to do the thing I loved.

As I continued these informal studies of the companies I worked for, there was one piece of the puzzle I couldn't figure out: marketing. It always looked like black magic to me. The high-priced marketing gurus where I worked spent tens of thousands of dollars of precious seed capital on advertising campaigns that were confusing, at least to me. So I began asking questions about the message, the artwork, the trade shows we attended, the brochures, the way we talked about ourselves as a company, the measurability of the efforts, and so on. The only responses I got from these geniuses was that I didn't understand marketing.

Shortly after we started Menlo, someone who knew my burning desire to understand marketing dropped off a couple of CDs titled *Monopolize Your Marketplace.* These former Madison Avenue marketing executives had me from their opening line: "Everything you know about marketing and advertising is wrong!" I knew it—and here were two actual marketing geniuses confirming it. There were many great lessons on these audio CDs, but the one that had the greatest effect on me was their admonishment to "align the world's outside perception of your company with your inside reality."

I had *never* seen a marketing campaign like that. The message felt quite freeing, because it meant you didn't have to lie to anybody about anything. The message you delivered to the world could be (and should be) the same message you deliver to your customers, your team, your family, the community, tour guests, interviewees, new hires, magazine writers, and everyone else your company comes into contact with.

There are three points that define the essence of a business: the world's outside perception of the company, the inside reality for the team that works there, and the heart of the leadership. Too often, these are not in sync, and actually are based on different values and practices.

You need to have an inside/outside perception that is in alignment, or is working to get back into alignment as quickly as possible. Visitors frequently tell me that they would never want the world to know their company's inside reality. This is incredibly sad to me. If they don't want people seeing inside their culture, their inside reality must not be that great. The hypocrisy will ultimately kill their company. Cynicism will overtake their culture, and their best people—those who authentically care—will leave. In contrast, once you have a system that is in alignment, or can work to get back into alignment whenever disturbed, you have a system that will right itself when it is knocked off balance.

Betting on Your Culture

One of the earliest business relationship traditions established at Menlo, conceived by cofounder and CFO Bob Simms, is what we call a "leveraged play." In this practice, we offer our clients up to a 50 percent cash deferral on our invoices in exchange for equity in our client's company or royalty in the product we are helping them bring to market. In some cases, we do both.

This simple strategy aligns every part of our joyful mission. A leveraged play is an open declaration that we intend to help our clients bring a product to market that will be widely adopted and enjoyably used by the people for whom it is intended. If we truly believe in our mission, our purpose, and our ability to deliver on it, why wouldn't we be willing to place a substantial bet on the outcome? We have done more than two dozen such investments so far in our history. Two have worked out to be big wins, one of them was huge, a couple of others were smaller returns, and at least three have gone out of business and won't be returning anything to us. The rest are still in play. Our leveraged-play board resembles a standard venture capital or angel investment portfolio. Ongoing royalties from previous work amount to around 15 percent of our annual revenue.

In February 2011, I received a call from Jeff Williams, the CEO of Accuri Cytometers, one of our major clients and a longtime partner in our leveraged-play business model. Jeff told me that Accuri had just been sold for $205 million to Becton Dickinson. A few months later, we received the biggest single payment in our company's history, given our leveraged-play trade for equity in Accuri. We took the team out for a dinner celebration and handed each of our Menlo employees the largest single checks they had ever received from us. It was a gratifying moment for the founders.

Tracy, one of our quality advocates and High-Tech Anthropologists, was sitting next to me, and I couldn't help but ask if this money was going to make a difference for her family. She turned her head away without saying too much. The next morning, I caught up with her and asked her again if this result was a good thing, telling her we appreciated knowing whether we are doing the right thing for our team. Again, she turned away from me. I apologized and said I wouldn't press any more. She assured me it was okay, but it was clear what she was about to share was deeply important.

From Tracy:

> **Unknown to Rich at the time of that team dinner, the team** had just promoted me to the senior level. At Menlo, you don't get promotions by sucking up to your manager, working extra hours, gaining hero status, or threatening to leave (as I've experienced elsewhere). You have to earn them. In fact, it is your peers who determine if you have earned them. For me, knowing that my peers had acknowledged my hard work as valuable enough to move me to a senior level was—well, even now I struggle for the right words.
>
> I felt honored.
>
> Don't get me wrong. I was stunned by the bonus, too. Even knowing that Menlo would be getting a big check, I was not prepared for how generous our bonus checks would be. But a bonus is a momentary thrill. The people I work closely with every day—the people I consider to be my extended family—made me a senior.
>
> Me.
>
> That was something I was going to have to live up to. That was something I was going to have to continue to earn every day. That was the most meaningful raise I had ever been given.
>
> Joy.

These kinds of stories give me chills when I think of the alignment it represents between the founders, the team, and our clients and the power that alignment has for all of us. I thought the alignment of sharing the financial rewards was a big deal, and I wanted to know how much of a difference it makes in the lives of our team and their families. What I heard from Tracy was far more powerful. She reminded me that the everyday belief system she shared with the team far outweighed financial outcomes. Her life had been more greatly impacted by her teammates than a big check being handed to her by the CEO.

Values at Work, Not on a Plaque

If you visit Menlo, you will see our values at work. You see the openness, the transparency; you feel the energy and hear the collaboration. If you attend our daily standup, you witness our democracy.

Values cannot exist solely for our own people but must be built into our contracts and business agreements as well. You can't preach the gospel of joy and then turn around and hand your client a manipulative deal, for example. We've heard more than once that our contractual terms are quite evenhanded and represent both signing parties. We have always felt that our contracts—whether with customers, employees, or subcontractors—should be ones we'd be comfortable signing no matter what side of the table we were sitting on. When we receive contractual terms from our clients, many of them are completely one sided; it is left as a difficult exercise for us to add in terms that protect our interests. We see this as incredibly wasteful and a terrible way to begin a relationship between two companies. Conversely, we have refused to do business with companies whose terms are too onerous or inconsistent with what we believe will produce joy. Most requests for proposals (RFPs) fall into this category. We see time and again companies creating a tight little box for their supplier by tricking them into committing to something that couldn't possibly work in the end. We usually politely decline to respond to RFPs. The RFP process is all about seeking the lowest-*priced* supplier, while we are typically the lowest-*cost* vendor. We often see the lowest-priced vendor produce software to the specification of the RFP, but the resulting software is unusable by the target audience. That is a really expensive way to save money. Our price is typically higher than our competitors, but as the software we build is actually used, cost per use—what we believe to be the true value of software—is very low. What we promise our clients must always be aligned with our personal and organizational pride.

Our values are reflected not only in our big, strategic business decisions and client dealings. We make it a point to honor our values in small ways as well. I recall one visitor who was touring on the Monday after our annual holiday celebration, when three hundred people had visited and partied with us. At our standup that day, I mentioned that we should find a way to thank the cleaning crew as they had gone above and beyond the call of duty to clean so thoroughly and thoughtfully after our messy party. Not two minutes after standup, Jeff J. announced a collection for the cleaning crew and raised three hundred dollars in short order.

That spontaneous, random act of kindness delighted our visitor. I suppose this moment reflected our core values in ways that have become so commonplace that it took an outsider to highlight for us what we value. Jeff assumed the role of leader after a simple report at standup; the team felt empathy for the hard work of the cleaning crew that had gone beyond its normal workload to provide us a clean and professional space. As I reflect on it now, I realize our cleaning crew cares about our culture just as we do, and so does McKinley, our landlord, who manages and selects this crew. When even your vendors want to align with your culture, you're on the right path.

We are also open to the press in ways that are probably unprecedented in most companies. Because everyone at Menlo is fully in alignment with our values and mission, we don't need a handler when the press arrives to take pictures or do a story. Everyone can attest to our culture as well as the CEO. Because of this, it is not unusual for writers to spend one or two days in our space simply observing and being a fly on the wall. The team doesn't change their behavior at all. When a magazine editor spent two days in our space, she even attended Tracy's feedback lunch.

Think of your own company. Would you let an outside visitor— let alone a reporter—sit in on your most confidential meetings? Would you be open to letting them hear you discuss budget concerns, staffing issues, personnel disagreements? If not, this points to the existence of certain practices and values you wish to hide from others, since they don't align with how you want the world to think about your culture. Instead of hiding your culture, change it.

Our values extend to our community interactions as well. We are fortunate to be in a vibrant downtown, near a college campus, with lots of energy. We teach and speak at the local universities and colleges, host community groups in our space, and sit on various non-profit boards. In turn, it is not at all unusual for us to host a university president, provost, or dean as they are seeking the same joy in their institutions that we've created in ours.

We extend ourselves to the community both as individuals and as a company. I often spend the first two hours of every day in coffee shops near our office so I can be accessible to a variety of community members on a very casual basis. I will also usually have several mentoring sessions a week with students and entrepreneurs in the community. Our values live on in our annual Menlo holiday party. Team members, customers, friends, family, and fans all come together to honor one another as part of Planet Menlo populated by Menlonians.

The Effectiveness of Alignment

Our focus on alignment creates interesting efficiencies. First off, we don't need or have a professional sales force. In general, the right kind of customers show up and the wrong ones don't. The community becomes our sales force. As so many in the community have visited Menlo or know a team member or have used our products, they *know* our culture. If they catch a hint of someone who needs software, they send him our way. They also probably coach him just a bit before he gets here, as most potential new clients arrive reasonably well schooled in our values.

This also affects recruiting. The community is our recruiting team. Because we've built great relationships with wonderful professors at the local and regional universities, the professors cherrypick the students they know would be the best fit. One professor at Oakland University, who has been to only one tour, has crafted a computer science curriculum around our practices. He invited me to judge a senior projects class. It became clear very quickly that he has elevated Menlo to hero status with his students. I had the same experience at UC Berkeley when my good friend Pat Reed, an adjunct professor there, invited me to an event with many of her students. As she introduced me around this Bay Area gathering, it was clear Pat had elevated me and our company to hero status. These same scenarios have played out in so many venues that résumés come in from everywhere unsolicited.

We have a sales and marketing force as large as the community we've touched and immersed ourselves in. It's crazy to consider how much attention a firm of our small size attracts. We could never afford this level of press if we hired a PR firm. Ironically, I've been invited to PR association events as a speaker to share our formula. One of my strongest pieces of advice? If the phone rings, answer it and be ready to tell your story. If you don't want to tell your story because the outside perception isn't in alignment with the inside yet, get it there—and then tell the world.

A joyful culture produces stories the world is yearning to hear. Capturing those stories and retelling them often reinforces your culture, as the outside world will want to come peek inside, ask probing questions, and walk away inspired to pursue their own joyful journey.

There is great power in a shared belief system and the stories it creates. It's equally important to be able to tell the story well. We are very proud of what we have accomplished in our intentionally joyful culture. But we are far from done. We must continually experiment and try new things—and solve the problems we do face.

FIFTEEN

Problems

Number 9. Success means you get better problems— but there will always be problems.

—ARI WEINZWEIG,

cofounder, Zingerman's,

"Twelve Natural Laws of Building a Great Business,"

A Lapsed Anarchist's Approach to Building a Great Business

After all this, *now* I start talking about problems?

Yes, we have problems. In fact, James and I can often be heard saying we have *all* the same problems anyone else has. That is a bit of an exaggeration. As I've said before, our phone doesn't ring off the hook with problems—in fact, it almost never rings with any problems.

However, it's not our goal to eliminate problems from ever occurring. If we really weren't having any problems, it would be because we've stopped running experiments, we've stopped growing, we've stopped learning. We would have stopped making mistakes.

What kinds of problems am I referring to? You know the list: a new hire who isn't adapting to our culture; gossip; not closing a deal; a philosophical difference between pair partners about how a feature should be implemented; a team member who moves faster than a pair partner; a pair partner who moves slower; a team member who dominates conversations; team members who are almost always silent even when they are concerned; those who think they should get raises just because they've been with us for a long time; those who should be getting raises but aren't because they have somehow slipped through the cracks in our feedback system . . .

Menlo is not perfect. Our code is not error free. Our designs can still frustrate some users. Our process isn't consistently well honed for every phase of every project. Our learning curve isn't always as smooth as we would like. Our hiring practices miss good people or sometimes bring mismatches on board whom we hang on to longer than we should. Interpersonal relationships within the team sometimes deteriorate. If someone is not performing quite up to team expectations, we might be caught beating around the bush rather than using direct conversation. Sometimes we are too direct and forget to empathetically consider the listener, or what our own role might be in the difficulty. Despite all of our conversations in our big open space, there is still at times the pernicious effect of harmful gossip. All of this is to say: we are human. Please forgive us.

Perhaps the key difference when any of this happens is that we know it and it bothers us enough to do something about it. These problems aren't seen as problems only *management* needs to fix. The team doesn't wait for an executive to offer solutions to problems; they go after these problems on their own with confidence. (Most of the time.)

I would also suggest that while we may have the same *number* of problems as everyone else, we do not have the same *size* of problems. This makes a huge difference. When we see a problem and correct it when it is small, we all feel empowered.

Real Problems at Menlo

When pressed about a specific problem we have yet to solve systematically and effectively, I can think of a few quite quickly. The first is communicable disease. When flu season hits, Menlonians drop like flies. We have antibacterial gel on every table, but we still get caught. It is one of the key disadvantages of our open work space and paired structure. Another is our dishwasher problem. One of the disadvantages of a big shared space is figuring out who needs to load and unload the dishwasher. Seriously. Just like at home, there are some who simply do it out of duty and some who sit back and let others do it. We had a "Menlo Mom" role once upon a time, and while she did a great job for us, it didn't seem like a very sustainable or professional solution.

These are small problems, but we also need to continue to experiment around some key areas in strengthening our team. Below are some of Menlo's current concerns and problem areas.

PROMOTIONS: We still haven't figured out a system we are all happy enough with here. It's still too haphazard. It is better than anything I've seen in my career, but it's not good enough yet. The beautiful thing about this problem is that the team is determined to solve it rather than simply complain about the system's not working well enough. Our reviews are peer reviews organized by the team member wishing to get feedback. Currently, we have three different pay grades at each of five different levels (Associate, Consultant, Senior Consultant, Principal, and Senior Principal). Our challenge is to figure out a more consistent approach that feels fair and is understandable to everyone. If someone wishes to increase his or her pay by moving from Associate III to Consultant I, it shouldn't feel arbitrary or inconsistent. The team has been organizing Lunch 'n Learns around this to explore the best way to provide consistency to our efforts without making it feel as if it's a stupid, standard annual review form from HR.

GROWTH: As we grow, we must change and adapt our systems, our practices, and even how we spend our time when it comes to coaching. I've noticed there are some myths that have developed at our current size that wouldn't have survived long when we were smaller. I heard, for example, one team member ask a question that I could have answered. When her peers suggested she talk to me, she said, "I couldn't talk to Rich. He's the CEO." Yikes! Another growth issue is that newer team members assume they don't have the same powerful voice as more seasoned team members when they feel something is going in the wrong direction.

DISTANCE: Our system works very well when our customers are in close proximity but is less optimal for our geographically distant clients. With our distant clients, we have established a practice of meeting in person at least once a month. In order to keep travel burdens to a minimum for both us and them, we alternate which side travels, keeping trips down to six per year for each team. In between, we continually experiment with electronic options. Our favorite so far is Google Hangout.

SHOES FOR OUR TEAM: You're likely familiar with the old saying about the shoemaker's kids not having any shoes. There are many technical things we have to do at Menlo to support our business, such as building, rebuilding, or improving our own Web site. We also have toyed with the idea of creating some of our own software prototyping tools to make the design of iPhone and iPad apps easier and faster. An obvious source of talent for these internal technical projects is our own team. This has proven to be historically difficult for us. We are so used to seeing internal projects as *bench* projects that can be cannibalized when paying projects need those team members, that internal projects are often viewed as second-class citizens. We have done several experiments but have yet to conquer this one.

What Do Emergencies Look Like at Menlo?

As I alluded to earlier, the last time we had a client emergency was in 2004. We were working on the organ transplant information system, and an organ became available one Saturday for a patient whose record was trapped and irretrievable in the system we were helping to build. The record was there, but the doctors couldn't pull it up.

Frantic calls were made to our switchboard and the hospital looking for the record. They eventually connected with one of our programmers at home, who manually retrieved the data to save the day and the patient. The experience shook us, and for a short time we considered using pagers to make sure we could provide an immediate response to such freak emergencies. But given that nothing of this magnitude or unexpectedness has happened again in the subsequent decade, we haven't gotten back to trying to solve this problem.

A more standard high-alert situation for us occurs when something significant happens to the flow and state of business. These moments usually occur when our system has failed to produce the next series of clients as other projects are winding down. This was particularly evident in 2008 when the Great Recession hit. We made varied attempts to get customers to start stalled projects during this time. We brainstormed clever pricing strategies that wouldn't tie us down for the long term. We invented the flexible deadline discount, offering our clients a 25 percent discount if we could determine their weekly budget based on our resource availability. If we had extra people available, we could increase their project team by a set amount, and if we needed extra staff for another client project, we could take a set amount away. A couple of our major clients took us up on this model. It reduced our revenue from individual clients but leveled our resource usage so that we could keep everyone busy during tough times.

In that tough economy, we also took some chances on clients that we otherwise would likely not have thought to work with. One of these clients was a sole proprietor whose company managed dog agility competitions; she needed software to track the nationwide data for her business and her customers. We had no idea this project and those that followed would produce such a great client relation-ship, as we typically deal with much larger organizations.

Then there was the emergency that happened when the economy turned back on like a spigot in April 2011, the beginning of the second quarter of the year. Clients we had been patiently checking in with since early 2008 were suddenly ready to press Play on their projects again—and they didn't want to wait. My impression was that large corporations that had been hoarding cash out of fear sud-denly got the green light to renew tech projects and were all ready to spend right away.

As most of our projects skew toward High-Tech Anthropology in the earliest stages, we were going to be well short of the people we needed for all the projects that were starting at the same time. We immediately picked several candidate team members from our pro-grammer, project manager, and QA pools, dubbed them High-Tech Anthropologists, and sent them on the road. We made some quick hiring decisions, too, including hiring one programmer's wife, who just happened to be in the room one afternoon. It was a crazy, high-energy time, and it was exciting to see how quickly the team could adapt to the sudden acceleration. Of course, our paired approach meant we could ensure the quality of practices during the spin-up phase. I was very proud of how the team turned up the dial in striv-ing to be good teachers to those joining the effort, and proud too of our new team members for being such good students.

Some describe these kinds of crises as "good problems to have." My take? Good problems are good problems for the first five minutes, and then they just feel like regular problems until you solve them.

The Role of Critics

Every leader has key critics, those who listen to all your rhetoric and stories and then poke telephone poles into the big, gaping holes in your arguments and hold you uncomfortably accountable.

You hope that if something you are doing is wrong, annoying, out of kilter with the culture, or perceived as any of those things, it will be brought to your attention—and sooner rather than later. As the CEO, even at a small company with a strong culture like ours, I will always get a slightly varnished form of the truth. It's part of human nature to filter what you tell "the boss." My first line of defense against this insular information-gathering system is to have my table out in the room with everyone else's. Still, I overhear only those conversations going on near me.

I need honest critics, and am lucky I have a few on the team. Unlike perhaps many of you, I have family members on my team. My wife, Carol, and all my daughters have worked at Menlo. My family typically does not hesitate to give me unvarnished feedback. However, they are not the only ones. My two business partners, James and Bob, and another former partner and friend, Tom, are always there to give me feedback as well.

Finally, some members of our team are great sounding boards because they know there's no retribution for criticism. I recall the time we were rolling out the idea of incubating start-up companies in our space. In my view, there were great opportunities in doing this, not the least of which was that we might be nurturing a new Menlo client that when it got big enough would need a software team. I thought it could be an exciting next step in our growth.

Kealy, Rob, and Jeff thought otherwise and let me know right in the middle of a meeting. They raised doubts during the Q&A of my presentation. Their concerns seemed unwarranted to me, and it kind of pissed me off that they weren't embracing my grand new idea, especially in front of the whole team. I responded as best I could during the meeting, but it was clear they weren't buying it. They were concerned that this experiment might dent our culture in ways we couldn't fully control, because we couldn't necessarily expect that a new company in our space would share the exact same belief system. We went ahead and ran a first experiment by incubating a single company. It turns out the dissenters were right. It was never quite as bad as they'd been fearing, but it was also not as good as I'd been hoping. The best part of all of this was that the three of them didn't hesitate to push back. It was a good lesson for all of us, including me.

In a trusting environment, criticism can take the helm and right the ship when things have the potential for getting off course.

Having honest critics is a good problem to have, even if it doesn't feel that way in the moment.

Stepping into Joy

A few years ago, AAA Life Insurance scheduled a series of training classes with us for its IT team. Seventy-five team members attended our classes in three separate groups. By the time the third group came through, it was obvious there had been some talk back at the shop about this crazy Menlo stuff. By the end of the third class, I could sense some raw emotion starting to spill out. I asked the AAA IT people in front of me what was going on.

"We don't understand why our management is sending us to these classes. This is a waste of our time and the company's money."

I asked them why they thought it was a waste of time. Their management team would never let them work the way Menlo does, they replied. If that's the case, I wondered aloud, why were they being sent to take our classes? Their question exactly.

"Have you asked them?" I inquired.

"Well, no."

"Go ask them," I implored. "In fact, you have my permission to go ask them. Blame it on me. Tell them you want to work like this. They will be shocked by the passion and energy you are bringing. They won't know what to do with it. Then tell them to come here to see me and take this class."

"Tell who?" they asked.

"The CEO, the CFO, the VP of marketing, the head of HR, everyone on the executive team. Tell them they need to come here," I said. What did I have to lose? The employees who had come to our session were excited and energized about the possibility of joy at work, perhaps for the first time in years.

"They will never come here," they lamented. "And they would never spend a whole day. They wouldn't care enough to spend that much time on this."

"Go ask them," I commanded. "Blame the request on me."

Within two weeks, I had the entire AAA Life Insurance senior management team at Menlo, sitting through the exact same eight-hour class. At the end of the class, their response was, "This is so cool. But our technical team would never go for this."

Boom! I had 'em.

They started tearing down the walls within weeks.

It has not been an easy transition for AAA, moving to a culture of our style of joy. There are still doubters, but there are now passion, energy, and ownership all around.

Every organization has invisible walls, walls that no one ever tests. Once tested, they can disappear like a morning fog.

Find Your Why

Every organization needs a vision, a *why*. Your personal *why* will emanate from your heart song. Watch Simon Sinek's *Start with Why* video, or read his book.

Some will try to tell you your *why* is about *success*. You think you'll be happy if you are "successful." "The Happiness Advantage" author, Shawn Achor, teaches that we have that success equation backward: we will be successful once we are happy. As you've heard me say, you will be successful once you achieve joy, which is even deeper and more meaningful than happiness. Your heart knows what gives you that feeling of joy. Listen to it.

Write Down Your Vision

Take a quiet hour to sit down with your computer, your tablet, or a pen and paper and describe a good day five years from now. Pick an exact day. Write down what is happening in your life on that day.

I'll give you the opening line:

It's June 1, 20XX, and today I . . .

Then start writing. The description should be dripping with detail. It should be both personal and global—it shouldn't be just about you; it should be about both you and the joyful results you are helping to produce in the world. It should reflect both your personal goals and your work goals.

What you write will blow you away, because it will be your heart writing, not your brain. The description will show what you *want to feel* rather than what you *want*.

In my own writing, this exercise revealed the depth to which I desire to be near my family and have them involved and supported through their own work within what we've created. It also highlighted my desire to allow uncapped professional and financial growth for Menlonians. Finally, it spoke to what I imagined was our role and responsibility to our community and the world.

Here is an excerpt from my first crack at it:

It's May 1, 2018, and I am putting together my talk for Inc. *magazine's Top Small Company Workplaces Conference. I am their keynote speaker. I will be discussing the theme from my soon-to-be released third book,* Inspired: The Joy of Entrepreneurship.

I am spending some time preparing for the Menlo retreat, a tradition started shortly after Joy, Inc. *was released in 2013. These now weeklong retreats have inspired some of Menlo's greatest new innovations. They have also been a great time to work on some of the finer aspects of Menlo's now world-famous culture.*

James will also be there. He and I continue to be best of friends and have deepened our business relationship through a number of serious business experiments that the world still thinks are crazy but that somehow always seem to work. Both James and I now enjoy single-digit golf handicaps.

The Menlo family of companies now commands over $60 million in total annual revenues. The company is still privately held, but profit sharing and a reverse leveraged-play model (in which Menlo team members trade up to 50 percent of their own income for a piece of the upside of the project they are working on) have created more than a dozen Ann Arbor multimillionaires, who, amazingly, stay with the company despite the fact that they are now financially independent.

Menlo now employs more than 350 people locally. However, our reach into the community is far deeper than the revenues and employment numbers suggest. Several of Ann Arbor's most successful entrepreneurs can trace their roots directly to Menlo. Some of them worked here. Some partnered with Menlo using the now famous leveraged-play model. Some were mentored directly by Bob, James, and me.

Menlo is very involved in the nonprofit community. There is barely a board in town that doesn't have at least one Menlonian. Many board chairs are Menlonians. Menlo is also the top sponsor of almost every nonprofit event in the community. This includes the human services sector as well as early childhood education and the arts community. More than one hundred Menlonians volunteer as

mentors in the local school systems. Menlonians also sponsor twenty
kids a year at Cornerstone Schools in Detroit.

Menlo is about to celebrate the graduation of its thousandth in-
tern. The Menlo internship program is now hailed by community
colleges and universities around the nation as a model for creating
the next generation of technology and design leaders.

This year's retreat is at our northern Michigan home on beautiful
Elk Lake. It will be a fun mix of work and pleasure. I will stay a
week after with Carol, the girls and their husbands, and my four
grandchildren. Next year will be even busier, with the two new ex-
pected arrivals.

Looking back, I see that every year I get closer to my vision. I'm on
track to build the company I want, which brings me the joy I outline
in this letter. What would yours say?

Try Small, Simple Experiments

To jump-start the exploration of joy in your own workplace, surprise your team with some simple experiments. Here are a few you
might consider. They won't cost anything.

WHERE DO YOU SIT? Most visitors are simultaneously intrigued
by and uncomfortable with the thought of a space without walls,
offices, cubes, or doors. As I mentioned earlier, our guests are
intrigued by the fact that I sit out in the room with everyone else.
This kind of managerial experiment builds trust, the kind that
comes from treating your team members like the adults they are.

Changing your seating is a simple experiment to run. If you are
a leader trapped in an office or caught by the trappings of an office,
turn the office into a conference room, grab a small table, and move

out among the rest of your team. Ask them to select the table's location. Tell them it's okay to move it whenever they like without asking permission. Post a sign-up sheet outside the new conference room that was your old office and let the team know it's available to anyone, first come, first served. Have them name the room.

You can always book the conference room yourself for those truly private conversations. I'm guessing you will be amazed at how few there are. If you are having a lot of private conversations, there is likely something else amiss with your team that requires deeper attention.

Remember my earlier admonition: *everyone* has to change in order for you to achieve the dramatic change you seek. This includes you. What's the worst that can happen?

TRY A STANDUP MEETING FOR A WEEK: Go back to chapter four and read about how we do our daily standup meeting. Try it for a week. Set a timer, pick a goofy token, and experiment with some silly traditions. Find something fun in your current culture and blend it in.

COME VISIT: There's one thing you have that I didn't: Menlo. Come visit, explore, ask questions, take pictures. You are welcome anytime. If you are in Ann Arbor, just stop in. Someone will show you around.

It Won't Be Easy, but It Will Be Worth It

Easy change is neither lasting nor meaningful. If you choose joy, know that you are at the first steps of an arduous journey, perhaps the equivalent of climbing Mt. Everest. Changing human behavior is one of the most difficult efforts you will ever undertake and, quite possibly, the most rewarding. There will be storms, setbacks, and disappointments. You will need others to join you, to help you when you falter or slip.

This journey to joy at work is personal. It has to be. You want a job or an organization that brings you joy. You want to enjoy that "good kind of tired" at the end of each day, knowing you made your life just a little bit better today. Along the way, you transform yourself into the person you've always dreamed you could be. You get in touch with what makes your heart sing and you draw others to your flame. Those closest to you start to notice a difference in who you've become.

You'll start to see joy, feel joy, and almost touch joy within your entire team. Everyone is now feeling his or her own version of what you are feeling. Together you begin to speak confidently about your culture, your values, and your mission. There's a unified purpose and a way to deliver it. Now nothing seems impossible.

Finally, with this journey, you see the change in the world. The customers you touch, the products and services you deliver, the community that interacts with you, the people who help you tell your story—they become part of the joy, too. They want to be you, they want to be with you, they ask you how to achieve the joy you've achieved.

More than anything, I wish you that joy.

The Inspiration

Discontent is the first necessity of progress.

THOMAS A. EDISON

Light Up the World

On October 21, 1879, Thomas Edison lit an incandescent lightbulb in his lab in Menlo Park, New Jersey. He wasn't the first to make a lightbulb, but he was the first to make it a sustainable and useful invention.

Edison didn't care about being first; rather, he worked diligently with his team to create a practical bulb that could be widely adopted and enjoyably used by everyone. He wanted to build a reliable overall system that could deliver that light. Providing light to the world in a systematic and lasting fashion required an entirely different kind of team and culture. In that little lab, one man and his team changed the world in ways that we are still feeling more than 130 years later.

Henry Ford, another great American innovator, and Thomas Edison were both of Michigan heritage. (Edison was raised in Port

Huron, where his family moved shortly after his birth in Ohio.) The two men were great friends. On October 21, 1929, on the fiftieth anniversary of the original event, Edison, seated beside his dear friend Mr. Ford, re-created that famous first lighting at a newly built historical park called the Edison Institute, in Dearborn, Michigan. Edison sat and admired his wonderfully restored Menlo Park "Invention Factory."

In creating the Edison Institute, Henry Ford desired to capture the places of history before they were lost for all time. To honor Edison and his team, Ford's crew carefully collected every artifact they could find in the ruins of the crumbling New Jersey lab. They numbered every brick and board and loaded them onto a train, carrying the dirt from underneath the building along with them, and transported it all across the country to carefully reconstruct the entire lab in an outdoor museum in southeast Michigan that would come to be known as Greenfield Village.

Any kid who grows up in southeast Michigan visits Greenfield Village at least once a summer. I certainly did. Greenfield Village is a testament to our nation's legacy of entrepreneurial innovation and ingenuity. Ford collected buildings and historical artifacts from around the country and preserved them for future generations. As William Pretzer wrote in *Working at Inventing: Thomas A. Edison and the Menlo Park Experience*, Ford's "goal was to create a museum that would not only record the past but would shape the future as well. It would use the past to encourage visitors, especially the young, to aspire to great achievements of their own."

I can offer my personal thanks to Henry Ford. His vision worked for me. Whenever I walked into that re-created Menlo Park lab as a kid, I got goose bumps. At eight years old, I didn't know exactly what had happened in this tiny little lab, but for some unknown reason it spoke to me. I wanted to work in such an exciting environment. Doing what? I had no idea.

Looking back at the dreams I had as a twenty-year-old University of Michigan computer science student who wanted to assemble a fun, energized, talented software team someday, I now understand that I was pursuing the goose bumps of that Menlo Park childhood experience. I wanted that kind of energy for myself and for others who would join me. More than two decades later, when I started giving tours at Interface Systems, I once again began to reminisce about those childhood dreams. I started embellishing the tours by saying that what people were seeing was very similar to what had happened in Edison's Menlo Park lab. At the time, I had very little idea whether that was true, as I was just working from my remembered eight-year-old's perspective of that place.

In 2001, when four of us were discussing forming the company, I again started to think about the Edison energy and my heart song connection to that place. However, this time I didn't just want to invoke Edison and Menlo Park as a fun story embellishment. I wanted his story to be right up front in our new company and the culture we would build. Menlo Park would be embedded in the *name* of the company. It would be on the Web site and every business card and brochure. Edison's story would become part of our culture.

Was I simply chasing a childhood fantasy? To be sure, I needed to investigate what exactly had gone on at Menlo Park, to see whether it was as fantastical as I had believed it to be when I was a kid. Once again, I began reading. Two books in particular caught my attention: Pretzer's *Working at Inventing* and Paul Israel's *Edison: A Life of Invention*. As I began to learn more about what had actually happened in that Menlo Park "Invention Factory," I couldn't believe how many parallels there were to my own journey. I have been fortunate not only to have since met Paul Israel and Bill Pretzer but now to count them among my good friends. That has provided me the benefit of being able to rely on their historical knowledge of the magic of Edison's Menlo Park experience.

Naming the company in honor of Menlo Park was more than appropriate; it was powerful. The energy, the camaraderie, the space, the process, the results that were all there then are now evident in our version of that lab. My inner eight-year-old couldn't ask for any more joy.

Joy at work.

Acknowledgments and Appreciations

To my family . . .

I now understand better than ever why authors are so grateful to their family members, as they are the ones left to pick up the pieces of your life that fall to the floor when you stop everything else to write a book.

To my wife—Carol, you always knew I had a book in me, and you supported me the whole way. I can't thank you enough for everything you've done in my life to have made *Joy, Inc.* possible, not the least of which was your instrumental leadership in keeping Menlo going flawlessly in my grand absence.

I remember as if it were yesterday the day when I came home from Interface Systems and told you I had lost my job. You asked me if I was unemployed, and I said, "No, I'm an entrepreneur now." I think you are finally getting comfortable with what that means. You stayed by my side on the entire roller-coaster journey.

To my daughters—Megan, your deep and abiding passion is a wonderful reflection of what you have seen in me. It is such a joy to watch. Your attempts to bring what you've learned at Menlo into your other jobs makes me so proud of your courage and tenacity.

Lauren, you and I both still share the dream of an "adventurous life." That can and should include your work life. I know you will make sure of that. Your enthusiasm for life, travel, and adventure inspires me.

Sarah, you challenge me to be the best I can be both at work and at home. Thank you. Your strength and endurance inspire me.

To my business partners . . .

In dreaming one day of starting a business, I always knew I wanted partners. I knew that a business partnership needs as careful a consideration as a marriage. It's certainly the case that I spend most of my waking hours with my business partners, originally James Goebel, Tom Meloche, and Bob Simms, now just James and Bob.

Tom—you inspired me at the perfect time in my life. The inspiration you gave me when I was in my darkest professional hour set me on a path that continues to this day. I'm so glad we still get to spend time together.

Bob—you have taught me so much, but perhaps no better lesson than that high ideals are possible even within the legal and contractual part of the business. Through your ethical approach to business, we have enjoyed a stellar reputation in every one of our business relationships. I sleep well at night knowing that our ethics are written into our contracts and our values are played out in our management.

James—you are my best friend. Words cannot express the joy you have brought to me through all of these years together. I plan to keep saying yes to you for the rest of my days. I think everyone longs to have a best friend like I have in you. None of this would have been possible without you.

And to the Menlonians, past and present—thank you for believing! A special callout to Lisa Ho and Tracy Beeson for their early help in reviewing my writing.

To friends . . .

There are so many friends that have had such great influence.

To Bob Nero—your gentle hand on my shoulder kept me going. Menlo wouldn't have happened without your influence and your leadership example in my life.

To Jennifer Baird—my best customer ever, my friend, my prayer partner.

To Kerry Patterson—your thoughtful friendship is beyond anything I could have ever hoped for. Thanks to you and all the fine folks at VitalSmarts and to Doug Finton and Josh Boyd at Vital Skills International, who introduced us.

To Eastern Michigan University professor Diana Wong—your love for James and me and your heart for our mission are the wind beneath our wings.

To Kathy Macdonald—for your friendship and encouragement in the early days. For opening your library to me, and thus opening my mind to possibility.

To author Karen Martin—thank you for insisting that I write this book and for the introduction to my agent, John Willig.

To my agent, John Willig—thanks for taking a chance on me!

To *Inc.* editor Leigh Buchanan—thanks for your passionate understanding of the crazy culture we've created and your ability to turn that understanding into beautiful *Inc.* cover stories.

There are so many who inspire me it would be difficult to name them all. Ari Weinzweig, Paul Saginaw, and so many others on the Zingerman's team, you are twenty years farther down the road than we are, so I am hoping we can continue to learn from you as we have already. Thanks for making Ann Arbor special. To all the fine folks at the University of Michigan Positive Organizational Scholarship group, thank you for bringing such an inspirational message to the world. And to all the authors represented in my reading list, you are my teachers. Thank you for taking the time to share your passions with the world. Thanks to my alma mater, the University of Michigan, for giving me the foundation. Go Blue!

To Linda Irvin . . .

An obvious question I can expect in the future is: So, Rich, if this pairing thing is so powerful, did you write the book with a pair partner? No, I didn't. However, in the latest stages of editing, the hardest part, the part where you turn a manuscript into a worthy book, I was in trouble. I could no longer see the forest for the trees, and I needed help. Linda came to my rescue. We spent the better part of two weeks together, side by side, pair editing. It was awesome. You made me a better writer. You made this a better book.

To Portfolio at Penguin Random House . . .

And finally, thank you to the wonderfully supportive team at Penguin Random House. First to Niki Papadopoulos. You saw something in that first meeting, and you took a chance on joy. THANK YOU. And also to Natalie O. Horbachevsky, my dedicated editor at Portfolio. Wow! I have a little box at home full of discarded exclamation points and quotation marks, all because you taught me how to be a better writer. Thank you for keeping my focus on the reader, and thanks for your steadfast dedication to quality. I was proud to always meet your deadlines because your professionalism inspired me to be a good pair partner to you.

To Mom and Dad . . .

I would like to add this last dedication to my loving parents. I learned unconditional love from both of you. Mike, Brian, and I could not have asked for a better family growing up. Even though you are both gone now, I know you are looking down on me with the same parental pride you had while living. When the paperwork came for the incorporation of our business, the birth date of Menlo was stamped on the documents: June 12, 2001. Mom, you would have been eighty-four years old that day. Dad, I will never forget how you wept upon hearing that news, knowing full well that Mom's love had reached down from heaven and touched us all in such a beautiful way.

Recommended Teachers

To start your journey to joy, you must become a student again. The best way I've found to learn is to grab books and listen to talks that inspire you. Don't assume you'll be inspired by my recommendations. The relationship between author and reader is very personal, as it is between speaker and listener. Find those that inspire you.

The Menlo Library

At Menlo, we have a pretty rocking library. The books themselves range across many disciplines including design, marketing, entrepreneurship, software development, organizational development, teamwork, history, and more. If a team member spots a book of interest, he or she asks for it and we order it, no questions asked.

When certain books become wildly popular at Menlo, we start ordering them in quantity. Lencioni's *Five Dysfunctions of a Team* and *Getting Naked* are two of our most reordered books. We have many copies of *The Design of Everyday Things* by Don Norman, as well as *The Inmates Are Running the Asylum* by Alan Cooper. Others that have been longtime hits are *Creativity at Work* by Jeff DeGraff and Katherine Lawrence, and Pine and Gilmore's *Experience Economy*. My personal favorites are anything produced by the team at

Zingerman's, including Ari Weinzweig's *Zingerman's Guide to Giving Great Service* along with his more recent series, *Zingerman's Guide to Good Leading.*

Our checkout policy is simple: take a book and keep it as long as you need it. Bring it back when you're done. This liberal lending policy also extends to the wider Ann Arbor community. On occasion, someone from the outside brings a book in they think Menlo would enjoy. I believe this is a natural outcome of abundance thinking.

If the reader finds real value in the book, we encourage them to hold a Lunch 'n Learn. Of course, this means that we all get even more value from the book, including the presenter.

Here are some of my favorites:

Extreme Programming Explained, by Kent Beck (First Edition)

Planning Extreme Programming, by Kent Beck

What Clients Love, by Harry Beckwith

First, Break All the Rules, by Marcus Buckingham and Curt Coffman

Small Giants: Companies That Choose to Be Great Instead of Big, by Bo Burlingham

The Innovator's Dilemma, by Clayton Christensen

The Inmates Are Running the Asylum, by Alan Cooper

Creativity at Work, by Jeff DeGraff and Katherine Lawrence

Management, by Peter Drucker

Refactoring: Improving the Design of Existing Code, by Martin Fowler et al.

Design Patterns, by Erich Gamma, Richard Helm, Ralph Johnson, and John Vlissides

Blink: The Power of Thinking Without Thinking, by Malcolm Gladwell

Innovate Like Edison, by Michael Gelb and Sarah Miller
  Caldicott

The E-Myth Revisited, by Michael E. Gerber
The Tipping Point, by Malcolm Gladwell
Monopolize Your Marketplace, by Richard Harshaw
IDEO Method Cards, from IDEO
Edison: A Life of Invention, by Paul Israel
The Click Moment, by Frans Johansson
The Medici Effect, by Frans Johansson
The Art of Innovation, by Tom Kelley
The Ten Faces of Innovation, by Tom Kelley
Changing the Way We Change, by Jeanenne LaMarsh
The Five Dysfunctions of a Team, by Patrick Lencioni
Getting Naked, by Patrick Lencioni
*The Toyota Way to Continuous Improvement: Linking Strategy
  and Operational Excellence to Achieve Superior Performance*,
  by Jeffrey Liker and James K. Franz
Crossing the Chasm, by Geoffrey Moore
The Death of Competition, by James F. Moore
The Design of Everyday Things, by Donald Norman
Crucial Confrontations, Kerry Patterson et al.
Crucial Conversations, Kerry Patterson et al.
Influencer, Kerry Patterson et al.
The Experience Economy, by B. Joseph Pine II and James
  Gilmore
A Whole New Mind, by Daniel Pink
*Working at Inventing: Thomas A. Edison and the Menlo Park
  Experience*, by William S. Pretzer
A Guide to the Project Management Body of Knowledge, Project
  Management Institute
Building the Bridge as You Walk on It, by Robert Quinn
Deep Change, by Robert Quinn

The Highest Goal: The Secret That Sustains You in Every Moment,
   by Michael Ray

Diffusion of Innovations, by Everett M. Rogers

Maverick, by Ricardo Semler

The Fifth Discipline, by Peter Senge

Start with Why, by Simon Sinek

Bury My Heart at Conference Room B, by Stan Slap

A Company of Leaders, by Gretchen Spreitzer and Robert Quinn

The Great Game of Business, by Jack Stack

Big Brands, Big Trouble: Lessons Learned the Hard Way, by Jack
   Trout

Differentiate or Die, by Jack Trout

A Lapsed Anarchist's Approach to Being a Better Leader, by Ari
   Weinzweig

A Lapsed Anarchist's Approach to Building a Great Business, by
   Ari Weinzweig

Zingerman's Guide to Giving Great Service, by Ari Weinzweig

TED Talks

"The Happiness Advantage," by Shawn Achor, TEDxBloom-
ington

"Learning from a Barefoot Movement," by Bunker Roy, TED
Global 2011

"How Great Leaders Inspire Action" ("The Golden Circle"), by
Simon Sinek, TEDxPugetSound

Index